BRAIN LAB
for Kids

Brimming with creative inspiration, how-to projects, and useful information to enrich your everyday life, Quarto Knows is a favorite destination for those pursuing their interests and passions. Visit our site and dig deeper with our books into your area of interest: Quarto Creates, Quarto Cooks, Quarto Homes, Quarto Lives, Quarto Drives, Quarto Explores, Quarto Gifts, or Quarto Kids.

Inspiring | Educating | Creating | Entertaining

First Published in 2018 by Quarry Books, an imprint of The Quarto Group, 100 Cummings Center, Suite 265-D, Beverly, MA 01915, USA. T (978) 282-9590 F (978) 283-2742 QuartoKnows.com

Quarry Books titles are also available at discount for retail, wholesale, promotional, and bulk purchase. For details, contact the Special Sales Manager by email at specialsales@quarto.com or by mail at The Quarto Group, Attn: Special Sales Manager, 401 Second Avenue North, Suite 310, Minneapolis, MN 55401, USA.

10 9 8 7 6 5 4 3 2 1

ISBN: 978-1-63159-396-3

Digital edition published in 2018

Library of Congress Cataloging-in-Publication Data available

Design: Samantha J. Bednarek
Photography: Amber Procaccini Photography // www.aprocacciniphoto.com

Printed in China

BRAIN LAB
for Kids

52 Mind-Blowing Experiments, Models, and Activities to Explore Neuroscience

ERIC H. CHUDLER, Ph.D.

QUARRY

CONTENTS

INTRODUCTION

RIDING A BICYCLE, learning a new language, catching a ball, reading a book: these activities and everything else we see, hear, feel, and do are made possible by the soft, whitish-pink substance inside our heads called the brain.

We take for granted many of the amazing things our brain does for us. Although scientists have made remarkable discoveries about how the brain works, there are still many mysteries about how the brain does its seemingly miraculous feats. This book will help you understand how the brain accomplishes many of its actions. You will do this mainly by experimenting, testing, and building.

Using This Book

CAREFUL SCIENTISTS take detailed notes about the experiments that they do in their laboratories. You should start a lab notebook as you use this book. The pages of your notebook should be bound and not just a loose collection of papers. If you run out of room in one notebook, get another one. Your notebook should include the name of the lab or experiment, the date and time you did the activity, the methods you used, any observations you made, the results you found, and a discussion of what you think your results mean. Your notes should have enough information so that someone else who reads your notebook can perform the exact same experiment and understand what you discovered.

Each lab in this book is divided into several sections. After the title of each lab, the approximate time it will take to do the lab is listed. The Materials section lists everything you need to complete the lab, and the Method section provides a step-by-step guide of the procedures and materials you will need to complete the lab. You may find a different way to do an activity, and that is fine, but make sure that you write down any changes to the method in your notebook. The science behind an experiment is explained in the What's Going On section. This section will provide you with a better understanding of your experimental results and observations. Brain Facts are some interesting, fun, and perhaps surprising bits of trivia related to each lab. Finally, Thinking Deeper has additional ideas to further your exploration of a lab. For example, you might find an experiment for a science fair competition, or maybe you are just curious to see what will happen and discover something new.

UNIT 01

THE NEURON

NEURONS (NERVE CELLS) are specialized cells in the nervous system. These microscopic cells are like little batteries because they are able to generate small amounts of electricity. To communicate with other nerve cells, muscles, or glands, neurons send electrical signals over short and long distances. Each part of a neuron has a special function to ensure that these messages are sent quickly and efficiently.

Most people have never seen a real neuron. Scientists must use microscopes to see neurons because these cells are so small. Drawings and photographs of neurons help other people understand the structure of these cells. Another way to understand what a neuron looks like is to build a model of one and hold it in your hand. That is what you will be doing in these first labs: you will be making models of neurons. Of course, your models will be many times larger than a real neuron.

Although books and websites have drawings of typical neurons, remember that neurons come in many different shapes and sizes. As you build your neuron models, think about what makes a good model. How realistic should your model look? Does your model have the correct proportions? Does your model show all of the important parts of a neuron? How might you improve the construction of the model? Are there other materials you could use to make a model?

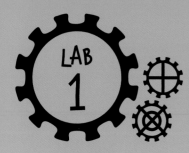

CLAY NEURON

BRAIN FACTS

→ The diameter of a neuron's cell body ranges from about 4 microns to 100 microns.

→ The axon of a neuron that stretches from the toe to the neck in a giraffe can be 14.8 feet (4.5 m) in length.

→ An octopus has about 500 million neurons in its nervous system. Most of these neurons are located in the octopus's arms.

The human brain contains 86 to 100 billion neurons (nerve cells). In this lab, you will create a model of a neuron using clay.

⏰ Time
→ 20 minutes

🔑 Materials
→ Modeling clay in 4 different colors

📝 Method

1. Gather small amounts of modeling clay in four different colors. Each color of clay will represent a different part of a neuron.

2. Roll the clay of one color into an acorn-size ball and then press it flat **(fig. 1)**. This piece of clay will represent the neuron's cell body.

3. With a second color of clay, add extensions to the cell body **(fig. 2)**. These extensions represent dendrites.

Fig. 1: Roll clay; press flat.

4. Roll a third color of clay into a thin line. Attach this piece to the cell body **(fig. 3)**. This new piece represents the axon of a neuron.

5. Press a small amount of clay of the fourth color onto the end of the axon **(fig. 4)**. This last piece of clay represents the synaptic terminal.

Fig. 2: Add extensions.

Fig. 3: Add axon.

Fig. 4: Add terminal.

THINKING DEEPER

Neurons can be grouped in different ways based on their structure and function. One way to group neurons is by their shape. For example, neurons that have many dendrites attached to a cell body are called multipolar neurons. Use clay to construct neurons with different dendritic patterns, such as unipolar, bipolar, and multipolar neurons. Another way to group neurons is by the direction they send information. Sensory neurons, for example, bring information from the senses into the central nervous system (brain and spinal cord). Motor neurons send signals out of the central nervous system to control muscles and glands. In between sensory and motor neurons are interneurons. Search the internet for examples of neurons found in different parts of the brain. For example, build a pyramidal cell from the cerebral cortex or a Purkinje cell from the cerebellum.

WHAT'S GOING ON?

A neuron (nerve cell) has four basic parts: dendrites, a cell body, an axon, and a synaptic terminal. Dendrites are connected to the cell body and take information to the cell body. The cell body (soma) contains the nucleus of the cell and other organelles necessary to keep a neuron healthy and functioning normally. A single axon attached to a cell body takes information away from the cell body. The end of an axon has a synaptic terminal that stores chemical neurotransmitters.

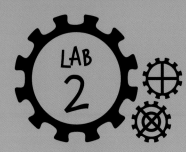

LAB 2

NEURO-SNACK

BRAIN FACTS

→ The word *nucleus* comes from the Latin word meaning "nut."

→ Some people around the world consider the brains of calves, goats, sheep, and squirrels to be a delicacy.

→ The brain has other cells called glia. Some glial cells provide physical support to neurons, bring fuel to neurons, or remove waste products.

Create this edible neuron to see the different parts of a neuron's cell body and then have a tasty snack.

⏰ Time

→ 30 minutes to prepare; 8 hours for the model to set

🔑 Materials

→ Mixing bowl
→ Spoon
→ 1 box of gelatin (any flavor)
→ Water
→ Cooking pot
→ 1 resealable plastic bag (sandwich size)
→ 1 can of fruit cocktail
→ Assortment of small candies

☢ Safety Tips

→ An adult should help with heating and pouring the hot water over the gelatin.
→ Beware of any food allergies.

Fig. 1: Mix gelatin and water.

✍ Method

1. In a mixing bowl with a spoon, combine the box of gelatin with the water by following the directions on the box **(fig. 1)**.

2. Let the gelatin cool to a warm temperature, and pour it into a small plastic bag **(fig. 2)**.

3. Drain the juice from the can of fruit cocktail. Add fruits and candy pieces to the bag of gelatin **(fig. 3)**.

4. Seal tightly and store the plastic bag in the refrigerator to set the gelatin **(fig. 4)**.

Fig. 2: Pour cooled gelatin into a small plastic bag.

Fig. 3: Add fruits and candy pieces to the bag of gelatin.

Fig. 4: Seal and refrigerate the bag.

Fig. 5: Once the gelatin is firm, remove and enjoy.

5. When the gelatin is firm **(fig. 5)**, open the plastic bag and remove the neuron model. Enjoy your neuro-snack!

THINKING DEEPER

What other foods could you use to make an edible neuron model? For example, make a neuron model using vegetables or breakfast cereal.

There are 86 to 100 billion neurons in the brain. Let's round up and assume that a brain has 100 billion neurons. If you tried to count all those neurons at a rate of one neuron per second, how long would it take? Yes, one answer is 100 billion seconds, but how many months or years is this? Do the math.

WHAT'S GOING ON?

Like other cells in the body, neurons are surrounded by a membrane. In your neuro-snack model, the plastic bag represents the membrane. The candy and fruit represent the nucleus, cytoplasm, mitochondria, and other organelles that contain genes, make proteins, and produce energy. Some of the organelles found inside the cell body of a neuron include

→ **Nucleus:** holds genetic material (DNA) to control the development of the neuron

→ **Nucleolus:** found inside the nucleus; helps build proteins

→ **Ribosomes:** helps build proteins

→ **Nissl bodies:** groups of ribosomes where proteins are made

→ **Endoplasmic reticulum:** system of tubes that transports materials inside a neuron

→ **Golgi apparatus:** wraps peptides and proteins into packages called vesicles

→ **Microfilaments and neurotubules:** give structural support to the neuron and help move materials throughout the cell

→ **Mitochondria:** create energy for the neuron

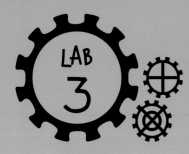

LAB 3

STRING NEURON

BRAIN FACTS

→ The brain of a honeybee has 950,000 neurons.

→ Neurons are the oldest cells in your body. Most of the neurons in your brain today are the same ones you had when you were born.

→ Neuroscience is the field that studies the structure and function of the nervous system.

It is not a parachute, a broom, or a tower. It's a neuron! A string neuron.

Time

→ **5 minutes**

Materials

→ **3 feet (1 m) of string**

Method

1. Tie the ends of the string to make a loop.

2. Place the string over your thumb and little finger of one hand **(fig. 1)**. If you are right-handed, use your left hand for this step.

3. Pinch the string in the middle of your palm and pull it down **(fig. 2)**.

4. Pinch the string in the middle of your palm again and pull it down again.

5. With your thumb and a finger of your right hand, reach into the loop **(fig. 3)** and place your fingers into the string on the thumb and pinky of your left hand.

6. Hold the string with your right-hand fingers and then pull the string out through the large loop.

7. Flip the string back over the three middle fingers of your left hand **(fig. 4)**.

8. Pull the string in the middle of your palm **(fig. 5)**.

Fig. 1: Put string over thumb/little finger.

Fig. 2: Pinch string and pull down.

Fig. 3: Reach into loop.

Fig. 4: Flip string back over.

Fig. 5: Pull string in middle.

WHAT'S GOING ON?

This string model shows a neuron's dendrites, cell body, axon, and synaptic terminal. Because this neuron model has many dendrites attached to the cell body, it is called a multipolar neuron. Scientists can use special chemicals to mark neurons so they can see the structure of these small cells. Some of these chemicals are absorbed into neurons while other chemicals are injected directly inside a neuron. Because neurons are so small, scientists must use microscopes to see and identify the different parts of a neuron.

THINKING DEEPER

Although this neuron model uses a thin string for its axon, real axons are so thin that you need a microscope to see them. Also, some axons are very long. For example, axons that have their cell bodies in your spinal cord can stretch all the way down to muscles in your foot. Make a scale model of a neuron by assuming that the cell body of a real neuron has a diameter of 100 microns and is connected to an axon that is 1 yard (m) long. If you used a ping-pong ball that has a diameter of 1.57 inches (4 cm) as the cell body, calculate how long the axon would need to be to maintain the same proportion as in a real neuron. Do the math and then tie a thread or string to the ball and stretch out the axon. How much thread will you need? Here is a hint: you are going to need a lot of thread!

PIPE CLEANER NEURON

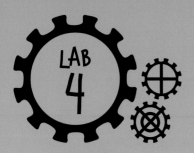

BRAIN FACTS

→ The distance between nodes of Ranvier is between 0.2 and 2 mm (0.02 and 0.08 inches).

→ Without myelin, electrical signals travel at speeds between 1.6 and 6.6 feet (0.5 and 2.0 m) per second or 1.1 to 4.5 mph (1.8 to 7.2 kmh). With myelin, electrical signals can travel at speeds between 16.4 and 393.7 feet (5.0 and 120.0 m) per second or 11.2 to 268.4 mph (18.0 to 432.0 kmh).

→ The word meaning *saltatory* comes from the Latin word meaning "to leap."

This simple model of a neuron (nerve cell) is made from pipe cleaners (chenille stems). Each stem color represents a different part of the neuron.

⏰ Time
→ **20 minutes**

🔧 Materials
→ **Scissors**
→ **Ruler**
→ **5 pipe cleaners (different colors)**

📝 Method

1. With scissors and a ruler, cut three of the pipe cleaners into 4-inch (10 cm) lengths **(fig. 1)**.

2. Place the remaining two long pipe cleaners to form a "+" sign **(fig. 2)**.

3. Bend one pipe cleaner in half over the other pipe cleaner **(fig. 3)**.

4. Twist this pipe cleaner to form a single length. This length represents the axon; the end of the axon represents the synaptic terminal.

5. Bend the cut pieces of one pipe cleaner around the untwisted pipe cleaner. These smaller pieces represent dendrites **(fig. 4)**.

6. Form a ball by wrapping a small pipe cleaner around itself. This represents the cell body **(fig. 5)**.

7. Twist more dendrite pieces onto the dendrites that are already attached to the cell body.

8. Wrap small pieces of a new pipe cleaner around the axon. This wrapping represents the myelin sheath **(fig. 6)**.

Fig. 1: Cut three pipe cleaners into smaller pieces.

Fig. 2: Form a "+" with two long pipe cleaners.

Fig. 3: Bend one pipe cleaner over the other and twist it around itself.

Fig. 4: Tie cut pieces around the untwisted pipe cleaner.

Fig. 5: Form a ball with the cell body pipe cleaner.

Fig. 6: Wrap small pieces of a new pipe cleaner or add beads to the axon to represent a myelin sheath.

WHAT'S GOING ON?

In addition to showing dendrites, a cell body, an axon, and a synaptic terminal, this neuron model has myelin. Myelin wraps around and insulates the axon of a neuron, helping send electrical messages more quickly through an axon. Instead of covering the entire axon, the myelin insulation has breaks called nodes of Ranvier. Electrical signals jump from node to node in a process called saltatory conduction.

THINKING DEEPER

Each neuron in the brain can be connected to thousands of other neurons. These connections, called synapses, form a network or circuit of interconnected neurons that processes information. Create a neural network with a wire mesh by threading your model neurons through the holes in the mesh. Leave a small space between the synaptic terminal of one neuron and the dendrites of another neuron for the synapse.

ROPE NEURON

BRAIN FACTS
→ The distance between a synaptic terminal and a dendrite is only 20 to 40 nanometers. (There are 1,000 nanometers in one micron and 1,000 microns in one millimeter.)

→ A single neuron can have from 1,000 to 10,000 synapses (connections) with other neurons.

→ One vesicle can contain 5,000 molecules of neurotransmitter.

Build a model of a neuron to show how an electrical signal travels down an axon and releases chemical messengers (neurotransmitters) at the synaptic terminal.

⏰ Time
→ 1 hour

🪝 Materials
→ Scissors
→ 10 feet (3 m) of thin rope
→ Drill
→ 3 plastic containers or bowls
→ 10 feet (3 m) of thick rope
→ 1 pool float
→ Wire cutters
→ 12 inches (30 cm) of wire
→ 10 ping-pong balls

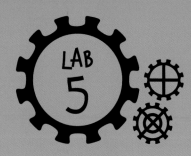

Fig. 1: Cut rope.

⚠️ Safety Tips
→ An adult should operate or supervise drilling holes.
→ Make sure that the person holding the container (synaptic terminal with the ping-pong balls (neurotransmitters) keeps his or her fingers and hands away from where the pool float comes into contact with the container.

📝 Method
1. With scissors, cut the thin rope into five 7-inch (18 cm) equal-length pieces **(fig. 1)**.

2. Tie a knot at one end of each piece of thin rope.

Fig. 2: Drill holes.

Fig. 3: Thread rope and knot.

Fig. 4: The knots should rest on the inside of the container.

Fig. 5: Thread thick rope through.

3. Drill five small holes around the rim of two plastic containers **(fig. 2)**. The holes on each container should be at the same place on each container because these will be wired together.

4. Drill five more holes through the bottom of one container. These holes should be large enough for the thin rope to pass through, but small enough so the knot in each rope will not slip through.

5. Thread each thin rope through a hole in the bottom of the container **(fig. 3)**. Pull the rope through the container completely so the knot rests on the inside of the container **(fig. 4)**.

6. Tie a knot in one end of the thick rope.

(continued next page)

WHAT'S GOING ON?

This model illustrates how neurons use electrical signals to communicate inside a single neuron and chemical signals (neurotransmitters) to communicate between different neurons. The thin ropes represent dendrites, the two containers wired together are the cell body, the thick rope is the axon, the open container is the synaptic terminal, the ping-pong balls are bags (vesicles) of neurotransmitter molecules, and the pool float is the electrical signal. When neurons communicate with each other using chemical messages, the neurotransmitters released from the synaptic terminal of one neuron float across a small gap before they attach themselves to special proteins (receptors) on other neurons. The area including the synaptic terminal, the gap, and a receptor is called the synapse. When neurotransmitters bind to receptors, they increase or decrease the likelihood that the receiving neuron will send an electrical signal.

ROPE NEURON (continued)

Fig. 6: Put float on rope.

Fig. 7: Wire container together.

7. Drill a hole in the center of the bottom of the other container with holes around the rim.

8. Thread the thick rope through this new hole **(fig. 5)**.

9. Thread the pool float onto the thick rope **(fig. 6)**.

10. Drill a hole in the center of the third plastic container.

11. Make a knot in the thick rope and then thread it through the center hole of the third container. The knot should be on the inside of the container.

12. Using wire cutters, cut the wire into 2-inch (5 cm) lengths.

13. Place the rims of the first two plastic containers so that the holes are side by side.

14. Thread a wire through the holes on each container. Tie the wires to seal the containers to create a boxlike shape **(fig. 7)**.

15. Place the ping-pong balls in the open container **(fig. 8)**.

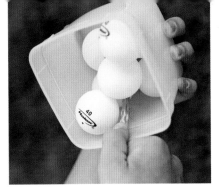

Fig. 8: Put ping-pong balls in open container.

Fig. 9: Send float.

Fig. 10: Watch balls go flying.

Fig. 11: Try to catch the balls.

To set up the model, different people should hold each of the thin ropes, another person should hold the open container with ping-pong balls, and another person should stand about 5 feet (1.5 m) away, facing the open container. Another person should hold the pool float near the sealed containers. Stretch the entire model so the ropes are tight.

To use the model, toss some ping-pong balls to the people holding the dendrites. This represents how neurotransmitters are released from a synaptic terminal and bind on receptors of a dendrite. When several balls are caught, the pool float should be thrown down the axon **(fig. 9)**. This represents how an electrical signal is sent through an axon. The pool float should hit the container with enough force to send the ping-pong balls flying through the air **(fig. 10)**. The person standing opposite the container should try to catch as many balls as possible **(fig. 11)**.

PASS IT ON

BRAIN FACTS

→ The diameters of axons range from 0.2 to 20 microns. The speed an electrical signal travels inside an axon depends on an axon's thickness. The thicker the axon diameter, the faster the signal travels.

→ Information about pain and temperature travels more slowly inside neurons compared to information about touch.

→ Some snakes have venom that blocks the chemical signal of one neuron from reaching the dendrite of another neuron.

Neurons can send messages at speeds up to 268.4 miles (432 km) per hour. Use a group of friends to send messages through a chain of neurons.

⏰ Time

→ 30 minutes

🔑 Materials

→ A group of at least 10 people
→ Small objects such as pebbles or coins; one object for each person
→ Stopwatch

📝 Method

1. Each person will represent a neuron. A person's arm will be a dendrite, his or her body will be the cell body, the other arm will be an axon, and that hand will be the synaptic terminal.

2. The small objects will be neurotransmitters.

3. People should line up side by side at arm's length from each other **(fig. 1)**.

Fig. 1: Line up.

4. Each person (neuron) should hold the object (neurotransmitter) in the same hand near the opposite hand of the person next to them **(fig. 2)**.

5. When someone says "Go," the person at the front of the line should drop the object into the hand of the next person **(fig. 3)**. Start the timer at this moment.

6. When the next person receives the signal, this person should drop his or her object into the hand of the next person in line.

Fig. 2: Hold small objects in one hand.

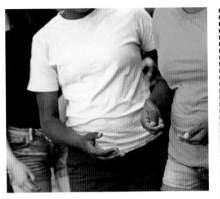

Fig. 3: Pass to the next person in line.

7. Continue to drop-and-receive down the entire chain of people.

8. The last person in the chain should say "Received" when the message gets to the end. Stop the timer to see how long it took the message to make it down the entire chain.

9. Remember, everyone has his or her own neurotransmitter at the start. This neurotransmitter is the one that each person should drop into the next dendrite. Each person should end up holding a new neurotransmitter that was received from the previous person.

WHAT'S GOING ON?

Messages travel through the nervous system using electrical and chemical messages. In this lab, each person became a neuron. To start a message, one neuron passed a chemical message across a small space. When the chemical was picked up by the dendrite of the next neuron, it created an electrical message that was sent to the cell body. From the cell body, an electrical signal (an "action potential") was sent down the axon to the synaptic terminal. To continue the message, the synaptic terminal released its own supply of neurotransmitters in a small gap across from the dendrite of another neuron. This model shows how a chemical message is used for communication between neurons and an electrical message is used for communication inside a single neuron.

THINKING DEEPER

The speed of an electrical signal can be measured if you know where and when the signal started and ended. To calculate the speed of the message in the chain of neurons in this lab, use a ruler to measure the distance from the first neuron to the last neuron. If you know the time it took the message to travel through the entire chain of neurons, you can do the math (distance ÷ time) to determine the speed of the message in your model. Compare the speed of the message in your model neuron chain to the speed of a message in a real neuron.

UNIT 02

THE BRAIN

RESTING COMFORTABLY IN YOUR SKULL, your brain controls everything you do. Your brain receives information from your senses to tell you what is happening in the outside world and from inside your body to help maintain your health. Your brain must understand this information and send commands to muscles, organs, and glands to act on the information.

You may not be aware of many of your brain's activities. For example, your brain controls your heart rate and breathing, but you do not have to think about making your heart beat or taking a breath. Of course, your brain helps with complex actions, such as reading, speaking, planning, and problem solving. Although scientists know how the brain does many of these complicated functions, they are still unraveling some of the mysteries about this 3-pound (1.4 kg) mass of tissue in our heads.

Labs in this section of the book will help you understand the structure of the brain. You will build models of the brain using different materials to show the anatomy of the outside and inside of the brain. The last lab in this section will show the importance of wearing a helmet to protect your brain. Remember that it is much easier to protect the brain from injury than to fix the brain after it is damaged.

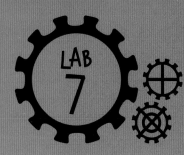

LAB 7

THINKING CAP

BRAIN FACTS

→ The cerebral cortex is made up of 41 percent frontal lobe, 22 percent temporal lobe, 19 percent parietal lobe, and 18 percent occipital lobe.

→ The total surface area of the cerebral cortex is about 324 square inches (2,090 cm²), or about the size of a full page of a newspaper.

→ The thickness of the cerebral cortex varies from 1/12 to 1/4 inch (2 to 6 mm).

→ The human cerebral cortex has 20 billion neurons.

Put on this "thinking cap" to show off the lobes of your brain.

⏰ Time

→ 3 hours over 2 days

🗝 Materials

→ Balloon
→ Papier-mâché paste. Pastes can be made using several different recipes:

- White glue and water (about 2 parts glue to 1 part water)

- White flour, salt, and water (about 1 part flour to 1 part water with a few tablespoons of salt)

- Liquid starch and white flour (about 2 parts liquid starch to 1 part white flour)

→ Mixing bowl
→ Scissors
→ Newspaper
→ Paints
→ Paintbrushes

Fig. 1: Make papier-mâché paste.

📝 Method

1. Inflate the balloon to a diameter about the size of your head.

2. Mix the papier-mâché paste in a large bowl **(fig. 1)**.

3. Cut the newspaper into strips 6 inches (15 cm) long and about 1 inch (2.5 cm) wide.

4. Dip the newspaper strips into the paste. Remove the excess paste from the newspaper strip.

Fig. 2: Apply newspaper to balloons.

Fig. 3: Draw the lobes of the brain onto the cap.

5. Apply the newspaper strips to the balloon **(fig. 2)**. Cover about half of the balloon from the top. Add enough layers of newspaper to give you a strong structure. Let the structure dry overnight.

6. Gently pry the newspaper mold away from the balloon. If needed, shape the edges of the mold and strengthen the sides of the cap with additional newspaper strips and paste for a good fit on your head. Let the structure dry again if it is wet.

Fig. 4: Paint the cap.

7. Draw **(fig. 3)** and paint **(fig. 4)** the "Thinking Cap" with different colors to show each lobe of the brain. If you need inspiration, refer to the illustration on page 29.

THINKING DEEPER

You can use your hands to outline the different lobes of the brain. To find your occipital lobe, interlock your fingers and then put your hands over your head, to a spot just above your neck. For the parietal lobe, raise your hands to the top of your head. Unlock your fingers and place them over your ears to find the temporal lobe. For the frontal lobe, place your palms on your forehead with your fingers pointing over the top of your head.

WHAT'S GOING ON?

The brain can be divided in half into a right side and a left side, or cerebral hemispheres. The wrinkles on the outside of each hemisphere are folds of brain tissue created by bumps (gyri) and grooves (sulci) in the cerebral cortex. The folding of the cerebral cortex increases the amount of brain tissue that can fit within the volume of the skull. Like fingerprints, the patterns created by sulci and gyri on the surface of the brain are different for each person.

The sulci and gyri also help define four different lobes within each cerebral hemisphere. As the name implies, the frontal lobe is located at the front of the brain. The frontal lobe is responsible for higher cognitive functions, such as reasoning and problem solving. Parts of the frontal lobe are also involved with movement and emotional behavior. The parietal lobe sits behind the frontal lobe and helps with the perception of information from the skin. Below the frontal and parietal lobe is the temporal lobe. The temporal lobe is involved with the perception of sound and the formation of memories. At the back of the brain is the occipital lobe, which is responsible for vision.

BUILD A BRAIN

BRAIN FACTS

→ *Cerebellum* is from the Latin word meaning "little brain."

→ The corpus callosum is a group of 200 to 250 million axons that transfers information between the right and left cerebral hemispheres.

→ The brain's right side controls movement and receives information from the left side of the body; the brain's left side controls movement and receives information from the right side of the body.

Build a brain model using clay.

⏰ Time

→ 30 minutes

🔑 Materials

→ Modeling clay in 6 different colors

✏️ Method

1. Gather small amounts of modeling clay in six different colors **(fig. 1)**. Each color of clay will represent a different part of the brain.

2. Shape the different pieces of clay into the four lobes of the brain, plus the cerebellum, and the brain stem **(fig. 2)**.

3. Press the different clay pieces together to create a single piece **(fig. 3)**. Reshape or add pieces of clay to form a brain with lobes in the correct proportions.

Fig. 1: Gather small amounts of modeling clay made in 6 different colors.

Fig. 2: Form the different pieces of clay into the four lobes of the brain, the cerebellum, and the brain stem.

Fig. 3: Press the clay pieces together to create a single piece. Reshape if needed.

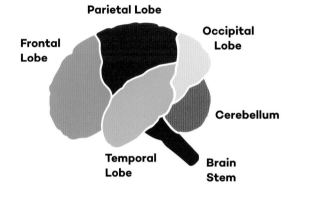

Parietal Lobe

Occipital Lobe

Frontal Lobe

Cerebellum

Temporal Lobe

Brain Stem

WHAT'S GOING ON?

In addition to the four lobes of the cerebral cortex, the brain has a cerebellum and a brain stem. The cerebellum is tucked under the occipital lobe and rests above the brain stem. The cerebellum is important for movement, balance, and posture. All information going up from the spinal cord to the brain and all information going down from the brain to the spinal cord must pass through the brain stem. The brain stem is composed of different structures that control breathing, arousal, heart rate, and blood pressure.

THINKING DEEPER

In this lab, you created a model of only one brain hemisphere. Now, build a brain model that has both hemispheres. Some brain structures cannot be seen from the outside. For example, the thalamus, corpus callosum, and hypothalamus are buried deep in the brain. Create a brain model that shows these and other structures you would see if the brain were split right down the middle.

What other materials can you use to make a brain model? Can you make a brain from recyclables or food? Create an entire brain with both right and left hemisphere and use materials with different colors to show different structures.

BAKED BRAINS

BRAIN FACTS

→ The average human brain is 5½ inches (14 cm) wide, 6.57 inches (16.7 cm) long, and 3⅔ inches (9.3 cm) high.

→ The average volume of the human skull is 7 cups (1,700 ml) of which the brain is 6 cups (1,400 ml), blood is ½ cup (150 ml), and cerebrospinal fluid is ½ cup (150 ml).[1]

[1] S. S. Rengachary and R. G. Ellenbogen, eds., *Principles of Neurosurgery* (Edinburgh: Elsevier Mosby, 2005).

Baked brains may look and smell tasty, but don't eat them.

⏲ Time

→ 1 hour

🔑 Materials

→ Oven
→ 2½ cups (270 g) flour
→ 3 tablespoons (50 g) salt
→ Mixing bowl
→ Spoon
→ ⅓ cup (75 ml) water
→ Cookie sheet
→ Paints
→ Paintbrushes

☢ Safety Tip

Be extremely careful using the oven. The cookie sheet and baked items will be *very* hot. Adult supervision is required!

📝 Method

1. Preheat the oven to 350°F (175°C).

2. Pour the flour and salt into a large bowl and mix them thoroughly with a spoon **(fig. 1)**.

3. Add water to the flour and salt and stir to combine. If the mixture is too crumbly, add a little more water **(fig. 2)**.

4. Spread some flour on a countertop or cutting board. Work the mixture into a ball and knead it on the countertop or cutting board **(fig. 3)**.

5. When the mixture can be molded, take a piece and form it into the shape of a brain. Place the finished brain on an ungreased cookie sheet **(fig. 4)**.

6. Bake the brain for 10 to 15 minutes. The brain might turn slightly brown, but do not let it burn.

Fig. 1: Mix flour and salt in a large bowl.

Fig. 2: Add water.

Fig. 3: Knead the mixture.

Fig. 4: Put the brains on a cookie sheet and bake them.

Fig. 5: Paint the brains using different colors for different lobes.

7. Remove the cookie sheet from the oven and let the baked brain cool to room temperature.

8. Paint the brain using different colors for the different lobes of the brain (fig. 5).

WHAT'S GOING ON?

When we are born, our brains weigh less than 14 ounces (400 g). As we get older, new connections are formed between neurons, and support cells (glial cells) continue to divide and multiply. By the time you are an adult, your brain will weigh about 3 pounds (1.4 kg) and make up about 2 percent of your total body weight. The baked brain you created is likely much smaller than a real brain.

THINKING DEEPER You can use the same flour, salt, and water recipe to make baked neurons. Remember to include dendrites, the cell body, the axon, and the synaptic terminal in your neurons. Both baked brains and baked neurons make unusual hanging ornaments. To create an ornament, make a small hole in your brain and neuron models before you bake them. When your models have cooled and you have painted them, thread a piece of string or wire through the hole to hang your new creation.

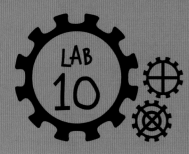

SPLASH DOWN

BRAIN FACTS

→ Cerebrospinal fluid (CSF) is produced by a structure called the choroid plexus.

→ People have ½ to ⅔ cup (125 to 150 ml) of CSF.

→ Between 1⅔ and 2⅛ cups (400 and 500 ml) of CSF are produced each day.

Build a model to show how the brain is protected by a layer of fluid.

⏰ Time

→ **30 minutes**

Materials

→ **2 raw eggs, in their shells**
→ **2 plastic containers with tops**
→ **Enough water to fill one container**
→ **Newspaper**

⚠ Safety Tip

Wash your hands after cleaning up a damaged egg.

Method

1. Place one egg into each of the containers.

2. Fill one container with water **(fig. 1)**. The other container should remain empty.

3. Close and seal the tops of both containers.

Fig. 2: Hold containers high.

4. Spread sheets of newspaper on the ground. The newspaper will help you clean up any mess you make.

5. Hold the container without water high in the air above the newspaper **(fig. 2)** and then drop it **(fig. 3)**.

6. Hold the container with water high in the air above the newspaper and then drop it.

7. Recover the containers, open them, and check for damage to the eggs **(fig. 4)**.

Fig. 1: Fill one container with water.

Fig. 3: Drop them.

Fig. 4: Check the eggs.

THINKING DEEPER Problems with the flow of CSF through the brain can occur if too much CSF is produced or if the circulation or absorption of CSF is interrupted. This may cause a buildup of CSF and an increase in pressure within the ventricles. This condition is called hydrocephalus, which affects approximately one million people in the United States. Symptoms of hydrocephalus include abnormally large heads, headache, nausea, movement and vision problems, seizures, and difficulty concentrating. Although there is no cure for hydrocephalus, the most common treatment for the symptoms is to place a shunt in the brain to direct the flow of CSF to another place in the body where it can be absorbed. Brain surgery can also be performed to create a pathway in the brain to allow the CSF to move or to burn the choroid plexus to slow the production of CSF.

WHAT'S GOING ON?

The brain (and spinal cord) is surrounded by a thin layer of liquid called cerebrospinal fluid (CSF). CSF also circulates inside the brain through a series of spaces called ventricles. This lab shows how CSF can protect the brain from injury. The plastic container represents the skull, the water represents CSF, and the egg represents the brain. It is likely that the egg in the container without water was cracked or broken when it was dropped, while the egg in the container with water was undamaged. This demonstrates that CSF can cushion the brain if the skull hits a hard object. In addition to protecting the brain from impacts, CSF allows the brain to float inside the head and reduces pressure to the base of the brain. CSF also helps clean harmful chemicals from the brain and transports hormones throughout the brain.

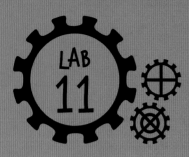

BRAIN PROTECTOR

BRAIN FACTS

→ In 1986, California was the first state to pass a bicycle helmet law.

→ In 2015, 817 bicyclists died in crashes with motor vehicles.

→ It is best to replace a bike helmet every three to five years. If a helmet is damaged, buy a new one rather than a used one.

Design and test a helmet to protect a model brain.

⏰ Time

→ 1 hour

🚀 Materials

→ 2 raw eggs, in their shells
→ 2 large plastic containers (such as clean yogurt containers)
→ Tape
→ Recyclable cushioning materials, such as packing peanuts and bubble wrap
→ Newspaper

📝 Method

1. Place one egg into an empty container and seal the top with tape **(fig. 1)**.

2. Pack recyclable materials into the second container.

3. Place the second egg into the packed container **(fig. 2)**.

4. Continue to pack recyclable materials around the egg.

5. Seal the top of the second container with tape.

6. Spread newspaper over the ground.

7. Drop the containers onto the newspaper **(fig. 3)**.

8. Open the containers and see if the eggs were protected.

9. Compare the damage done to each egg **(fig. 4)**.

Fig. 1: Place egg in container.

Fig. 2: Place second egg in padding material.

Fig. 3: Drop containers on newspaper.

Fig. 4: Compare damage.

THINKING DEEPER What makes an effective helmet and how could you improve the design and testing of a helmet? Think about the materials that you used to build your helmet in this lab. What would you change to make a better helmet? How would you design a larger helmet and test it for its ability to protect someone's head? Remember that a human head, including the brain, weighs 7.7 to 12.1 pounds (3.5 to 5.5 kg) and has a volume of about 17 cups (4 L).

WHAT'S GOING ON?

In this lab, you tested the effectiveness of a model helmet to protect the brain. The helmet was built from the container and insulating materials, the skull was the eggshell, and the egg yolk and white were the brain. Did your helmet protect the "brain" or was there some damage? In real life, helmets significantly reduce the risk of brain injury in case of a bike, skateboard, ski, or skating accident.

Bicycle helmets have three main parts: the outside shell, the inside liner, and a strap. The shell is usually a thin plastic layer attached to the inside liner. The layer of foam that makes up the inside liner is the most important part of a helmet because it absorbs energy from an impact. Straps and buckles hold the helmet on a bicyclist's head in the correct position. Helmets are tested by dropping them upside down from a measured distance. If the acceleration inside the helmet is within acceptable limits, it passes the test.

For maximum safety, a helmet should fit properly and stay in place when your head moves around. Helmets can be adjusted with foam pads or a fitting ring. Always buckle and tighten the strap snugly against your chin.

UNIT 03

REFLEXES

REFLEXES ARE QUICK, automatic movements that protect you from injury or help you maintain your posture and position. These involuntary movements occur in response to something in the environment and do not require conscious thought or decision making. For example, if your fingers touch something sharp or hot, you will move your hand away from the object before you even realize that you have done something dangerous. Reflexes that happen below the neck do not even need the brain to get involved. Instead, the pathways of neurons responsible for spinal reflexes stay in the spinal cord.

During a physical examination, doctors often test a person's reflexes to make sure nerves and muscles work properly. The strength of a reflex can help a doctor know what part of the nervous system is damaged.

In the following labs, you will test different reflexes. Don't worry if the responses you see are different from what happens in the doctor's office.

BRAIN FACTS

→ In bright light, the diameter of the pupil ranges in diameter from 1/12 to 1/6 inch (2 to 4 mm).

→ In the dark, the diameter of the pupil ranges in diameter from 1/6 to 1/3 inch (4 to 8 mm).

→ Humans have round pupils, but other animals have pupils with different shapes. For example, the pupil of a horse is a horizontal slit and a cuttlefish pupil is shaped like a "W."

Use your eyes to see how other eyes respond to light.

⏰ Time
→ 15 minutes

🦜 Materials
→ Flashlight

☢ Safety Tips

Light from the flashlight should sweep quickly across the eye of your test subject. Do not keep the light shining into the eye for a long time.

📝 Method

1. Dim the lights in a room.

2. Have a test subject sit in the dim room for about 5 minutes.

3. Look at the eyes of your test subject **(fig. 1)** and note the size of this person's pupil (the black center spot in the middle of the eye).

4. Shine a flashlight quickly across the eye of your test subject and observe what happens to the pupil **(fig. 2)**.

Fig. 1: Look at eyes; note pupil size.

Fig. 2: Shine flashlight to observe.

WHAT'S GOING ON?

When the room is dim, a person's pupil should be large. This allows more light to enter the eye so a person can see. When light from the flashlight moves across the pupil, the pupil gets smaller automatically because bright light can damage the eye. The automatic closing of the pupil is called the pupillary response.

THINKING DEEPER

This lab showed that light entering the eye on one side causes the pupil on that same side to get smaller. Test the effect of shining light into the eye on one side on the size of the pupil on the opposite side. For example, shine light into the left eye and see whether the size of the pupil on the right side changes. The pupil on the right side should get smaller. This response is called the consensual pupillary light reflex. Both pupils change size because information about light from one eye goes to both sides of the brain and signals from the brain go back to the muscles controlling the size of the pupils of eyes.

BRAIN FACTS

→ For the knee-jerk reflex, it takes only about 50 milliseconds (0.05 second) from the time of the tap to the start of the leg kick.

→ The first reflex hammer was developed by J. Madison Taylor at the Philadelphia Orthopedic Hospital in 1888.[2]

Has your doctor ever tapped on your knee during a checkup? In this lab, you become the "doctor" and test the reflexes of other people.

⏰ Time

→ **20 minutes**

⚲ Materials

→ **Large rubber eraser**
→ **Handle from a large mixing spoon**
→ **Rubber bands**

🗒 Method

1. Make a reflex hammer by attaching the eraser to the spoon handle with the rubber bands **(fig. 1)**.

2. Have your test subject sit in a chair so that his or her legs can swing freely.

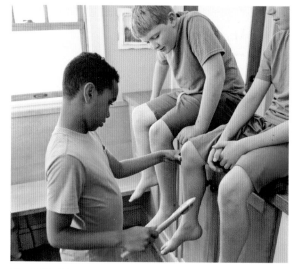

Fig. 2: Feel knee cap.

Fig. 1: Make hammer.

[2] D. J. Lanska, "The History of Reflex Hammers," *Neurology* 39 (1989): 1542–1549.

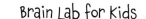

Fig. 3: Notice soft spot.

Fig. 4: Tap subject's knee.

3. Feel your test subject's knee below the kneecap **(fig. 2)**. Notice the location of a soft spot **(fig. 3)**.

4. Tap the soft spot below the test subject's knee with the reflex hammer **(fig. 4)** and observe the response of the leg.

THINKING DEEPER The brain is not required for the knee-jerk reflex because the reflex pathway involves only nerves and the spinal cord. However, the brain can still influence the knee-jerk reflex if someone thinks about stopping the leg movement. For example, if you tighten up your thigh muscle, your knee-jerk reflex may be smaller. To prevent conscious control over the reflex, try the Jendrassik maneuver. To perform the Jendrassik maneuver, have your test subjects interlock the fingers of their hands. As you are performing the knee tap, tell your subjects to pull on their hands. Compare the knee-jerk response before, during, and after the Jendrassik maneuver. Often, the Jendrassik maneuver causes a larger knee-jerk response.

WHAT'S GOING ON?

The knee-jerk reflex is called a monosynaptic reflex because there is only one synapse in the circuit needed to complete the reflex. The tap below the knee causes the thigh muscle to stretch. Information is then sent to the spinal cord. After following one synapse in the ventral horn of the spinal cord, the information is sent back out to the thigh muscle, which then contracts.

Doctors examine a patient's knee-jerk reflex to test for problems in the nerves, muscles, and brain. A weak or absent knee-jerk reflex could indicate problems with the leg muscle, the nerve bringing sensory information from the muscle to the spinal cord, or the nerve from the spinal cord telling the muscle to move. If the leg continues to move back and forth after the knee tap, there could be a problem with the patient's cerebellum.

CATCH ME IF YOU CAN

BRAIN FACTS

→ The ulnar nerve, radial nerve, and median nerve are the main nerves of the hand.

→ The human hand has twenty-seven bones.

Test your visual response time by catching a falling ruler.

Fig. 1: Hold the ruler and let it hang down between the thumb and first finger of your test subject. Tell your subject you'll drop the ruler in the next 5 seconds.

⏰ Time
→ 45 minutes

🚀 Materials
→ Ruler
→ Paper
→ Pencil or pen

📝 Method

1. Hold the ruler near the end (highest number) and let it hang down so the bottom edge is between the thumb and first finger of your test subject. The ruler should not touch the hand of your test subject **(fig. 1)**.

(continued next page)

💡 THINKING DEEPER

This lab tested visual reaction time. When your test subjects saw the falling ruler, they had to make a conscious decision to catch it. You can also test auditory (hearing) and tactile (touch) reaction times using this same experimental setup. To test auditory reaction times, ask your test subjects to close their eyes. Now when you drop the ruler, you must say "drop." When your test subjects hear the word "drop," they have to catch the ruler. To test tactile reaction time, again have your test subjects close their eyes. This time when you drop the ruler, tap lightly on your test subject's foot. When your test subjects feel the tap on their feet, they must catch the falling ruler. Compare the reaction times on the visual, auditory, and tactile tests and explain your results.

Try the experiment in a dimly lit room and compare the reaction time to the results you obtained in the bright room. If there is a difference in reaction time, how do you explain the results? Test different groups of people to determine who has the fastest reaction times. You might compare the reaction times of boys and girls or kids and adults. You should also try the experiment with a longer delay between the start time and the drop time. For example, you might tell your test subjects that you will drop the ruler within 10 seconds instead of 5 seconds. This added delay might prevent your test subjects from predicting when you will drop the ruler.

CATCH ME
IF YOU CAN (continued)

Fig. 2: Drop the ruler and record the number of inches (cm) where your test subject caught it.

2. Tell your test subjects that you will drop the ruler sometime within the next 5 seconds and that they must catch the ruler **(fig. 2)**.

3. Drop the ruler and then record the number of inches (cm) where your test subject caught the ruler **(fig. 3)**.

4. Convert this distance into a reaction time using the chart or the formula on page 45.

5. Test your subject four or five times by varying the delay in dropping the ruler. This will prevent your test subject from guessing when the ruler will fall.

6. Calculate the average reaction time for each test subject. See example data table on page 45.

Fig. 3: Calculate the average reaction time for each test subject.

WHAT'S GOING ON?

This experiment involved more than a reflex because it required conscious thought. To catch the ruler, your test subjects had to make a conscious decision to move their hands and close their fingers around the falling ruler. This lab measured the reaction time needed for visual information (the movement of the ruler) to travel from the eyes to the brain. The brain had to process this information and then send a motor command ("grab that falling ruler") to the muscles of the arms, hands, and fingers. If all went well, your test subjects caught the ruler.

DISTANCE CONVERSION TABLE

DISTANCE	TIME	DISTANCE	TIME
2 inches (5 cm)	.10 sec	4 inches (10 cm)	.14 sec
6 inches (15 cm)	.17 sec	8 inches (20 cm)	.20 sec
10 inches (25 cm)	.23 sec	12 inches (30 cm)	.25 sec
14 inches (35 cm)	.27 sec	16 inches (40 cm)	.29 sec
18 inches (45 cm)	.30 sec	20 inches (50 cm)	.32 sec
22 inches (55 cm)	.34 sec	24 inches (60 cm)	.35 sec
26 inches (65 cm)	.36 sec	28 inches (70 cm)	.38 sec
30 inches (75 cm)	.39 sec	32 inches (80 cm)	.40 sec

You can calculate the response time more accurately using this formula, where t = time (in seconds), y = distance (in cm) and g = 385.8 inches/sec^2 (acceleration due to gravity).

$$t = \sqrt{\frac{2y}{g}}$$

UNIT 04

TASTE

TASTE, AS WELL AS SMELL, are two senses that can detect chemicals in the environment. Taste relies on your sense of smell. For example, when you raise your fork or glass, small molecules travel up to the receptors in your nose. Taste receptors can detect chemicals from foods and drinks that you put in your mouth. The taste of foods can signal good things or bad things. It can help you enjoy a freshly baked cookie or warn you not to swallow spoiled milk.

There are hundreds of little bumps on your tongue called taste buds. Taste buds contain between 50 and 150 receptor cells each. These cells respond to the five basic tastes: sweet, sour, salty, bitter, and umami (or sa-vory), and provide the information that will be received by the brain. Someone might enjoy spicy food while a different person might pre-fer mild food, or sweets over savory snacks.

People prefer certain foods over others because of the brain's response to these signals. Information about taste is sent from the receptors to the brain through both the facial nerve and the glossopharyngeal nerve. These nerves receive and send the information from the tongue as well as from receptors on the cheeks and palate. The labs in this section explore the relationship between taste and smell and how your taste buds react to certain textures and colors of food and drink.

BRAIN FACTS

→ Information about taste from the tongue is sent to the brain by two nerves: the facial nerve (front two-thirds of the tongue) and the glossopharyngeal nerve (back one-third of the tongue).

→ The hypoglossal nerve controls tongue movement.

→ Foods with chemicals that activate umami receptors include soy sauce, Parmesan cheese, and mushrooms.

Investigate the importance of your sense of smell to your sense of taste.

⏰ Time

→ **15 minutes**

🪶 Materials

→ **Knife**
→ **Apple and pear**
→ **Blindfold**

☢ Safety Tips

→ **Beware of food allergies.**
→ **Wash the fruit and your hands before you cut the fruit with a clean knife.**
→ **Get an adult to help you use the knife.**

📝 Method

1. Using a knife, cut an apple and a pear **(fig. 1)** into 20 small bite-size pieces (10 apple pieces, 10 pear pieces).

2. Blindfold your test subjects.

Fig. 1: Cut apple and pear into 20 pieces.

3. Give one piece of fruit to your test subjects and have them taste it **(fig. 2)**.

4. Ask your test subjects whether the food is an apple or a pear.

5. Record the answer as correct or incorrect.

6. Repeat the experiment until your test subjects have tried 5 apple pieces and 5 pear pieces.

7. Now ask your test subjects to pinch their noses closed and to breathe through their mouths **(fig. 3)**.

Fig. 2: Give subject fruit to taste.

Fig. 3: Pinch nose and repeat.

8. Repeat the tasting experiment with the remaining apple and pear pieces.

9. Record whether your test subjects identified the apple and pear pieces correctly or incorrectly.

10. Compare your results from the two conditions.

THINKING DEEPER Make the experiment more difficult for your test subjects by using more than two different foods. For example, you could use different flavors of baby food or jelly beans. Make sure that your test foods have the same texture to avoid giving your test subjects any additional information about the identity of the food. You could also try clear liquids by adding salt, sugar, or lemon juice to water. Compare the ability to taste the difference between these liquids when your nose is open and closed.

WHAT'S GOING ON?

Your tongue is covered with tiny bumps called taste buds. Within each taste bud are 50 to 150 receptor cells that respond best to one of the five basic tastes: sweet, sour, salty, bitter, and umami (or savory). These receptor cells can respond to all of the five basic tastes, but they respond best to a particular taste. Responses from all receptor cells provide the brain with information about taste.

The sense of taste is highly dependent on the sense of smell. When you put food into your mouth, small molecules from the item travel up to special receptors in your nose. After these molecules get into your nose, they dissolve in mucus so they can attach to the receptors. When the chemical molecules bind to receptors, the receptors send electrical signals through a nerve to your brain. When your nose is closed, the airflow to the receptors in your nose is blocked. Therefore, you do not have information about smell to help you identify the food and the taste of food is blunted. This is the same reason why food does not taste very good when you have a cold with a stuffy nose.

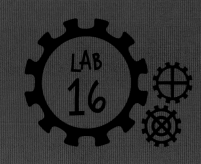

TASTY VISIONS

BRAIN FACTS

→ Taste buds are found not only on the tongue but also on the cheeks and palate.

→ The feet of a butterfly have receptors that detect chemicals. In other words, they taste with their feet.

→ An earthworm has chemical receptors all over its body.

Explore how vision influences your perception of taste.

Fig. 1: Mix drinks.

⏰ Time

→ 1 hour

🔧 Materials

→ 4 different powdered drinks, each with a different color
→ Measuring cup
→ Water
→ Clear cups
→ Food coloring (to match one powdered drink color)

📝 Method

1. Mix each drink according to the directions on the package **(fig. 1)**.

2. Pour ¼ cup (60 ml) servings of each drink into different clear cups **(fig. 2)**.

3. Pour ¼ cup (60 ml) of water into another clear cup.

Fig. 2: Pour water or clear soda into clear cups.

Fig. 3: Add food coloring.

Fig. 4: Ask subject to identify flavor.

4. Add a few drops of food coloring to the water **(fig. 3)**.

5. Ask your test subjects to try each drink and then identify the flavor of each **(fig. 4)**.

THINKING DEEPER If none of your test subjects was fooled by the unflavored, colored drink, change the test by diluting the flavored drinks and trying the experiment again. The diluted drinks will have a weaker taste and may help change the perception of the unflavored drink.

Food and drink companies spend millions of dollars to study how the color of food influences what it tastes like. Companies want to know how consumers perceive their products and they are always looking for ways to make their products more appealing to consumers. If changing the color of a food or drink can sell more product, you can be sure that the company will make the change.

People like to eat foods that have the color they expect. Over time, people learn that particular foods should be particular colors. Check the label on packaged foods to see what artificial colors are added to different products.

WHAT'S GOING ON?

Were any people fooled by the colored, un-flavored drink? Some people may have said that the unflavored drink tasted like one of the other drinks. Scientists are interested in this type of experiment to show how vision interacts with taste and smell. When people become familiar with certain combinations of colors and tastes, they learn to expect that foods with a particular color will have a specific taste. Therefore, learning can change our perceptions.

Taste **51**

WET OR DRY

BRAIN FACTS

→ Humans have approximately 10,000 taste buds.

→ Ageusia is the inability to taste anything; hypogeusia is a reduced perception of taste; hypergeusia is the enhanced ability to taste.

→ The length of a giraffe's tongue can be almost 2½ feet (74 cm).

→ Taste buds are replaced about every two weeks.

Find out whether you can taste anything with a dry tongue.

Fig. 3: Try to identify food by taste.

⏰ Time

→ **15 minutes**

🪝 Materials

→ **Foods such as sugar, salt, and crackers**
→ **Clean paper towels**
→ **Water (for rinsing your mouth in between tests)**

📝 Method

1. Dry the top of your tongue with a clean paper towel **(fig. 1)**.

2. Place a small amount of food on your tongue **(fig. 2)**.

3. Try to identify the food by taste alone **(fig. 3)**.

Fig. 1: Dry tongue with paper towel.

Fig. 2: Place food on tongue.

4. Rinse your mouth with water and then dry your tongue again.

5. Try different foods.

6. Repeat the test, but keep your tongue wet **(fig. 4)**.

Fig. 4: Repeat with different food.

WHAT'S GOING ON?

When your tongue is dry, the food will not have much flavor. You likely will not be able to taste the food because the chemicals in food must be dissolved to stimulate a receptor. When you dry your tongue, you are removing saliva that would dissolve the chemicals. When your tongue is wet, chemicals from the food dissolve and can bind to taste receptors.

THINKING DEEPER Many books and websites have pictures of a tongue map that shows where salty, sweet, sour, and bitter taste buds are located. Test the accuracy of these tongue maps by applying drops of salty, sweet, sour, or bitter liquids or foods on your tongue. Compare the location where you can taste these items with the locations shown on a tongue map. You may be surprised when you find your tongue map is different from the ones you see in books. The typical tongue map in textbooks is wrong because receptors for all tastes can be found on all parts of the tongue.

UNIT 05

SMELL

YOUR SENSE OF SMELL, also known as olfaction, is the other sense that can detect chemicals in your environment. You are able to pick up on them as they float in the air and into your nose. Like taste, smells can be either pleasant or might help you avoid unsafe foods, drinks, and environments. Smell can allow you to enjoy the aroma of a freshly baked cookie or alert you of smoke from a fire. Some smells may trigger a memory, helping you remember people and places from the past.

When the chemicals from the environment enter your nose, they dissolve in a layer of mucus on the olfactory epithelium, which is a membrane in your nose. When you pinch your nose closed, the airflow to the receptors in your nose is blocked, which is why you are not able to smell anything. After they dissolve, the chemicals attach to hair cells, or receptors, on the olfactory epithelium, that are connected to axons. These axons send electrical signals to the olfactory bulb, which sends the information to the brain. The labs in this section explore how your sense of smell works as well as how taste and smell work together to help the brain form a full picture of an object.

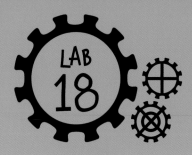

LAB 18

WHO SMELLS?

BRAIN FACTS

→ Humans have about 40 million olfactory receptors; German shepherd dogs have 2 billion olfactory receptors.

→ People who have no sense of smell have a disorder called anosmia.

→ The smell of green bell pepper can be detected when it is mixed with air at only 0.5 part per trillion.

Humans can distinguish thousands of different smells. In this lab, you will investigate the sensitivity of your sense of smell.

⏱ Time

→ **30 minutes**

✂ Materials

→ **Perfume or cologne**
→ **Containers, such as used yogurt cups**
→ **Measuring cup**
→ **Water**
→ **Marker**
→ **Lab notebook**

✏ Method

1. Add one drop of perfume or cologne to a container **(fig. 1)**.

2. Add ¾ cup (180 ml) of water to the container **(fig. 2)**.

3. Label the bottom of the container with a letter. Make a note in your lab notebook of this letter and the number of drops in the container.

Fig. 1: Add one drop perfume.

4. In a new container, add three drops of perfume and ¾ cup (180 ml) of water. Again, label the bottom of the container with a letter and the number of drops of perfume.

5. Continue to make different solutions by adding more drops of perfume, but always add the same amount of water. Make at least five different solutions. Remember to label the bottom of the container and record the "code" in your lab notebook.

6. When all of your solutions are made, you are ready to start the experiment. Place the containers in front of your test subjects and

Fig. 2: Add water to perfume.

Fig. 3: Order containers by smell.

Fig. 4: Check labels.

ask them to order the containers from the weakest smelling to the strongest smelling **(fig. 3)**.

7. After your test subjects have ordered the smells, look at the label on the bottom of each container to see whether they ordered the cups correctly **(fig. 4)**.

WHAT'S GOING ON?
Your sense of smell (olfaction) requires that chemicals floating in the air make their way into your nose. For you to detect these chemicals, they must dissolve in a layer of mucus on a membrane in your nose called the olfactory epithelium. After they dissolve, the chemicals attach themselves to receptors (hair cells) on the olfactory epithelium. The receptors are connected to axons that send electrical signals to the olfactory bulb. From the olfactory bulb, information is sent to several areas of the brain, including the olfactory cortex, hippocampus, amygdala, and hypothalamus, that help us understand the meaning of the signals.

THINKING DEEPER Examine your data to determine whether your test subjects were able to order the different solutions correctly. If the solutions were not ordered correctly, check to see whether your subjects made mistakes in the same place. Also, check to see whether people had more trouble with repeated attempts to order the solutions. Does the ability to smell get better or worse when people have more time to smell each solution? If the test was too difficult for your subjects, make the solutions more different from one another by adding more drops of perfume or cologne to adjacent containers.

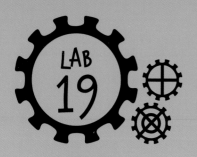

LAB 19
SCRATCH-AND-SNIFF CARDS

You may have seen scratch-and-sniff perfume cards inserted into magazines. Now you can make your own.

BRAIN FACTS

→ Natural gas is normally odorless. Mercaptan is the chemical that gives natural gas its rotten egg smell so people can detect gas leaks.

→ The chemical butyl mercaptan gives skunk spray its stinky smell.

Fig. 1: Crush spices and flowers.

Fig. 2: Mix with glue.

Fig. 3: Place mixed glue on index card.

Fig. 4: Let the glue dry.

⏰ Time

→ 1 hour

🖌 Materials

→ Scissors
→ Paper, cardboard, or index cards
→ Dried herbs such as oregano, basil, rosemary, and dill
→ Spices such as cinnamon and cloves
→ Flowers
→ Glue

📝 Method

1. Cut the paper into 2 by 2-inch (5 by 5 cm) squares.

2. Mix an herb, spice, or crushed flower **(fig. 1)** with a few drops of glue **(fig. 2)**.

3. Place the mixed glue on the paper **(fig. 3)**. Let the glue dry **(fig. 4)**.

4. Scratch the dried glue and smell the card.

❓ WHAT'S GOING ON?

Scratching the glue releases molecules of chemicals from the trapped herbs, spices, and flowers. The chemicals can then float in the air into your nose, where they bind with receptors.

THINKING DEEPER Many brain areas that receive information about smell are part of the limbic system. The limbic system is important for emotional behavior and memory. Because of the close association between smell, emotions, and memory, some smells can remind you of people, places, and events from the past. As you go about your day, think about the smells you come across and the memories that they produce. You might trigger a strong memory when you smell a particular flower or freshly baked cookies.

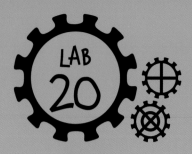

SMELLY T-SHIRTS

BRAIN FACTS

→ Sweat is made mostly from water with small amounts of fat, sodium, potassium, and calcium.

→ Humans have 2 to 4 million sweat glands on their body.

→ Sweat glands are found all over the body except on the lips and inside the ear canals.

→ Mosquitoes are attracted to body odor.

Take the smelly T-shirt challenge in this lab.

⏰ Time

→ **5 days**

🔑 Materials

→ **5 T-shirts (same style, same color)**
→ **5 large plastic bags (big enough to hold the T-shirt)**
→ **Masking tape**
→ **Marker**

📝 Method

1. Provide a T-shirt to five different test subjects who know each other **(fig. 1)**.

2. Ask your test subjects to wear the T-shirt for 1 hour on five consecutive days **(fig. 2)**. They should not wash the shirt at any time.

3. On the fifth day, the test subjects should put their shirts into plastic bags and return them to you **(fig. 3)**.

Fig. 1: Provide shirts to subjects and label with codes.

4. Label the bags with a special code, using masking tape and a marker, so only you know the person who wore the shirt.

5. Mix up the bags and then ask your test subjects to use their sense of smell to find their own shirt and to identify the wearers of the other shirts **(fig. 4)**.

Fig. 2: Ask subjects to wear shirts for an hour each day.

Fig. 3: Have shirts returned in plastic bags.

Fig. 4: Try to identify shirts by smell.

 THINKING DEEPER Compare the ability of family members to identify the shirts of their relatives to those of other people. The result of this experiment might tell you whether people who are related to each other or live in the same house smell the same. If the shirt smells are not strong, ask your test subjects to wear the shirts for a longer period of time or exercise while wearing the shirts.

WHAT'S GOING ON?

The T-shirts absorb the body odor of the wearer. The smell of each person is unique because it is influenced by sweat, diet, soap, shampoo, and medications. Sweat is produced by skin glands and helps maintain body temperature. Body odor is produced when sweat mixes with bacteria on the skin. Most people find it easy to identify their own T-shirts but have trouble matching other people to their T-shirts.

MAKE PERFUME OR COLOGNE

BRAIN FACTS

→ Early perfumes used whale vomit and animal urine.

→ A perfumer is someone who creates perfumes.

→ Some perfumes can cost more than $100 for only 1 teaspoon (5 ml).

Make your favorite scent with one of these recipes.

⏰ Time

→ 30 minutes

🔑 Materials

→ 7 tablespoons (100 ml) water
→ Mixing bowl
→ Fresh flower blossoms
→ Paper coffee filter
→ Vanilla extract
→ Ground cinnamon
→ Cloves
→ Container or spray bottle to hold the mixture

📝 Method

RECIPE 1

1. Pour the water into the mixing bowl **(fig. 1)**.

2. Add a handful of freshly chopped flower blossoms to the water **(fig. 2)**. Flowers with strong smells such as lilac, lavender, orange blossoms, and honeysuckle work well.

3. Let the flower/water mixture sit overnight **(fig. 3)**.

4. Strain the water through a coffee filter into a clean container or spray bottle **(fig. 4)**.

5. Squeeze the coffee filter to get out all of the liquid.

Fig. 1: Add water to a bowl.

Fig. 2: Add chopped flowers or cinnamon and cloves.

Fig. 3: Let sit overnight.

Fig. 4: Strain through coffee filters.

RECIPE 2

1. Pour the water into the mixing bowl.

2. Add a dash of vanilla extract, a pinch of cinnamon, and a few cloves to the mixing bowl.

3. Let the mixture sit overnight and then strain it through a coffee filter into a clean container or spray bottle.

4. Smell the water. If you need more of one ingredient, add it, and let it sit, then filter it again.

WHAT'S GOING ON?

Chemicals in the flowers, herbs, and seasonings dissolve in the water. When the chemicals are released from the water, they drift in the air, and if they make it to your nose, you have a good chance of smelling them. Cosmetic companies spend millions of dollars each year to create new perfumes to appeal to consumers. The smell of some perfumes may be attractive to some people, but other people may find these same perfumes unpleasant.

THINKING DEEPER

Make new perfumes with spices and herbs such as mint, rosemary, and orange peel. Although a bit expensive, essential oils from many different plants can be used to make perfume. Some essential oils that make nice perfumes include lemon, cedarwood, bergamot, vanilla, anise, peppermint, and lavender. You need to add only a few drops of essential oil to the water for a strong smell.

UNIT 06

VISION

YOUR EYES ARE THE WINDOWS to the outside world. Even in a darkened room, or with starlight at night, your eye's photoreceptors, or the cells within the innermost layer of the retina, send information from the outside world about light's brightness to your nervous system, allowing your brain to then process the information. Once the brain processes the information from your receptors, you're able to recognize people and objects with just a quick glance. You can identify the shape, size, distance, movement, and color of an object all within a span of milliseconds from the time your eye receptors first receive the information until you see and recognize the image. With this information from the receptors, you can easily identify the face of a friend in school, estimate the speed of a car driving past you, and appreciate a fine work of art.

The labs in this section explore how the receptors in your eyes work, how your brain understands the information it receives from those receptors, and the sights and images you're able to see as a result of this lightning-quick process. You will also discover examples of visual illusions to show how the brain makes assumptions about what you see and how the process of viewing an image is not always as simple as it may seem. You will be amazed to find out that it is very easy to fool your brain.

BRAIN FACTS

→ An adult human eyeball is just under 1 inch (2.5 cm) long; a baby's eyeball is ⅔ inch (16.5 mm) long.

→ A human eye weighs about ¼ ounce (7.5 g).

→ The lens of the eye is ⅙ inch (4 mm) thick.

→ There are no nerves or blood vessels in the lens of the eye.

Model the lens of your eye with a magnifying glass.

⏰ Time

→ 30 minutes

Materials

→ Tape
→ White paper
→ Magnifying glass
→ Pencil

Method

1. Tape a white piece of paper to a wall that faces a window. The wall should be about 16½ feet (5 m) from the window.

2. Hold the magnifying glass about 4 inches (10 cm) from the paper **(fig. 1)**.

3. Move the magnifying glass back and forth to focus the image from the window **(fig. 2, fig. 3)**.

4. Draw the image on the paper and compare it to what you see out of the window **(fig. 4)**.

Fig. 1: Hold magnifying glass around 4 inches (10 cm) from paper on wall.

Fig. 2: Move it to focus image.

Fig. 3: Observe the objects outside the window.

Fig. 4: Can you see that they're inverted on the paper?

THINKING DEEPER

Small muscles attached to the lens can contract to flatten the lens. This action changes how light passes through the lens and can help focus light on the retina. People are nearsighted when light is focused in front of the retina so that distant objects look fuzzy. Glasses with concave lenses will help correct the vision of people who are nearsighted. If light is focused behind the retina, people are farsighted and will need glasses for reading. Glasses with convex lenses can help people who are farsighted see close-up objects clearly.

Experiment with different lenses and magnifying glasses. Compare the distances needed to focus light on the paper with the different lenses. Also, examine what happens to the image when light passes through the lens at an angle.

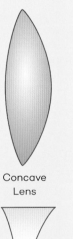

Concave
Lens

Convex
Lens

WHAT'S GOING ON?

The light we see is just a small portion of the existing electromagnetic radiation in our environment. This energy travels in the form of waves. We can see this type of energy when it has wavelengths between 380 and 760 nanometers because we have special cells (photoreceptors) in the retina of our eyes that respond to those wavelengths.

The image you see projected on the paper should be an inverted image of whatever is outside of the window. Light coming through the lens of the magnifying glass is projected onto the paper upside down and right is changed to left. This is what happens when light passes through the lens of your eye and is projected onto your retina. Photoreceptors in the retina respond to light and send electrical signals to the brain. The brain is able to make sense of these signals and understand that right is really left and up is really down.

BRAIN FACTS

→ This lab is named the Stroop Effect after J. Ridley Stroop, who discovered this effect in the 1930s. The original description of the Stroop Effect is online at http://psychclassics.yorku.ca/Stroop.

→ The cingulate area of the brain responds when people try the Stroop test.

Use this lab to demonstrate how the color of a word can influence your ability to read a word.

⏰ Time
→ **30 minutes**

🔑 Materials
→ **2 pieces of paper**
→ **Colored markers**
→ **Timer**

📝 Method

1. On one sheet of paper, use the markers to make two lists of color names **(fig. 1)**.

2. For the first list, use the same color marker for the word of that color **(fig. 2)**. For example, write the word *RED* with a red marker and *GREEN* with a green marker.

3. For the second list, write the words with a color different from the word **(fig. 3)**. For example, use a green marker to write the word *RED* and a blue marker to write the word *GREEN*.

Fig. 1: Use colored markers to make a list of color names.

4. Now, read the lists out loud. Time how long it takes you to say the *color* of the words **(fig. 4)**. Do not read the words. Instead, say what marker color was used to write each word. For example, if a red marker was used to write the word *GREEN*, you should say "red."

5. Compare the amount of time it took you to say the colors in each list.

Fig. 2: For the first list, use the same color as the word.

Fig. 3: For the second list, use a different color than the word.

WHAT'S GOING ON?

For most people, it is more difficult to say the colors when the color of the word is different from the written word. This shows how one function (reading words) can interfere with another function (saying the colors). The difficulty may occur because you can read words faster than you can name colors. Alternatively, you might have trouble naming colors because it requires more attention than reading words.

Fig. 4: Time each other reading the lists and compare.

THINKING DEEPER

Change the word lists in different ways to see whether you can read the list faster. What happens if you turn the word lists upside down or rotate them 90 degrees? Make a third list of color words, but spell the color words backward. For example, use a green marker to write "DER," which is "RED" backward. Try a list of words that are not colors. For example, use different color markers to write words such as *book*, *cat*, *car*, and *sky*. Is it easier to say what color was used to write the words in these new lists?

BRAIN FACTS

→ The octopus, squid, and cuttlefish do not have a blind spot because their photoreceptors are on the innermost layer of the retina.

→ The optic nerve contains about 1,200,000 axons.

→ The retina ranges in thickness from 100 to 230 microns.

Find the blind spot (optic disk) on the retina of your eye.

 Time

→ 30 minutes

Materials

→ **Paper**
→ **Black markers**
→ **Ruler**

Method

1. Draw a small circle on the left side of the paper and an X on the right side of the paper similar to this image **(fig. 1)**. The circle and the X should be separated by about 6 inches (15 cm).

2. Hold the paper at arm's length in front of you. The middle of the paper should be lined up with the middle of your face.

3. Close your right eye **(fig. 2)**.

4. With your left eye, look at the X. Looking at the X with your left eye, you should still be able to see the circle in your peripheral vision.

Fig. 1: Draw a circle and an X about 6 inches (15 cm) apart.

5. Slowly bring the paper toward your face while you are looking at the X **(fig. 3)**. Keep looking at the X with your left eye.

6. At some distance from the X to your face, the circle will disappear.

7. If you move the paper closer to your face, the circle should reappear.

Fig. 2: Hold paper; close one eye.

Fig. 3: Bring the paper toward you.

THINKING DEEPER

If you close one eye, keep your head still, and look into the distance, you will not notice your blind spot. Certainly light is landing on your blind spot, but you see an uninterrupted scene. This occurs because your brain fills in the gap made by your blind spot. Experiment how your brain creates a complete scene by putting other images into your blind spot. For example, instead of a circle on the left side of the paper, draw a thick line extending from the X. Leave a gap in the line and then repeat the blind spot test. What happens when the gap is placed in your blind spot?

What if part of the line after the gap is a different color?
Now what happens when the gap is placed in your blind spot?

Make other patterns to test your brain's ability to complete a scene. Try these patterns and then make your own original patterns for your blind spot test.

WHAT'S GOING ON?

The retina of the eye has several different layers of cells. The innermost layer of the retina contains cells (photoreceptors) that respond to light. There are two types of photoreceptor cells. Rod photoreceptors respond to low light, shape, and movement. Cone photoreceptors work in bright light and provide information about color and detail. There are three different types of cones that respond best to a specific frequency of light.

Photoreceptors are connected to cells in other layers of the retina. Axons from the last layer of the retina collect in a location on the retina called the optic disk, or blind spot. This area has no photoreceptors because it is occupied by the optic nerve that sends signals from the retina to the brain. So, when you are moving the paper back and forth in front of your face, you are moving the image of the circle over the retina. When the projected image falls on the optic disk, you cannot see it because there are no photoreceptors to respond to the light.

BRAIN FACTS

→ The retina in the human eye has about 120 million rods and 6 million cones.

→ A person who is color blind is missing one or more types of cone receptors.

→ Approximately 8 percent of all men and 0.5 percent of all women are color blind.

Investigate how your ability to identify colors changes in low light.

⏰ Time

→ **30 minutes**

🖌 Materials

→ **5 different color cards, such as paint sample cards (free from paint stores), pieces of construction paper, or colored sticky notes**

📝 Method

1. Ensure that each card is the same size. Cut the cards to make them the same size, if necessary.

2. Write a different number on the back of each color card starting with 1 **(fig. 1)**.

3. In a well-lit room, identify the color on each card **(fig. 2)**. Record the number and the color.

4. Shuffle the color cards so they are no longer in the same order.

Fig. 1: Write number on each card.

5. Go to a partially dark room or dim the lights in a room **(fig. 3)**. Repeat the color card identification activity in a dark room. The room should not be completely dark and you should still be able to see a little.

6. Compare the color matches you made in the bright and the dark rooms **(fig. 4)**.

Fig. 2: Identify colors.

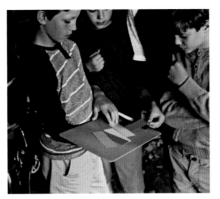

Fig. 3: Go to a dark room.

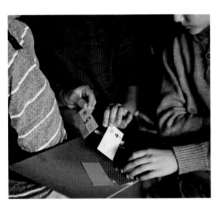

Fig. 4: Repeat color identification.

WHAT'S GOING ON?

Although you were able to see motion and shape in the dark, it is likely that you had trouble naming the colors in the dark. Remember that the cone photoreceptors in the retina respond best to a specific frequency of light and, therefore, send information about color. However, cones need bright light to work properly. In low light conditions, the other type of photoreceptor called rods takes over. Rods respond to changes in light intensity and provide information about movement and shape but not color. So, in the dark, you can see the shape of a card, but not its color.

THINKING DEEPER

It takes a few minutes for your eyes to adapt in the dark. Investigate the timing of adaption by testing your ability to detect color in the dark at different times after you enter a dark room.

Many people, especially men and boys, are color blind. The most common type of color-blindness affects a person's ability to distinguish between red and green. Repeat the color card experiment using different shades of red and green. You may also find Ishihara color-blindness test patterns on the internet to investigate color-blindness.

SIDE-CENTER TESTER

BRAIN FACTS

→ Humans have three types of cone receptors that are most sensitive to wavelengths of light responsible for red, green, and blue.

→ In addition to having eight legs, some spiders have eight eyes.

→ The eye of a dragonfly can have 30,000 lenses.

Compare the ability to see movement, color, and detail as images move from the side to the center of your vision.

⏰ Time
→ 30 minutes

✂ Materials
→ Pencil
→ Protractor
→ White paper
→ Glue
→ Cardboard
→ Colored markers
→ Craft sticks
→ String

✎ Method

1. With a pencil, trace the outline of the protractor onto a piece of white paper **(fig. 1)**. Glue the paper to cardboard and let it dry.

2. Label the protractor tracing with the degrees around the arc **(fig. 2)**. This will be your "tester."

3. Use a colored marker to write a letter or number on one end of a craft stick **(fig. 3)**.

4. Hold the tester level, up to your

Fig. 1: Trace protractor.

face, so the middle of the tester is in the middle of your head, just below your eyes.

5. Looking straight ahead, hold the craft stick to one side of your head along the outside edge of the tester.

6. Keep looking straight ahead and move the craft stick slowly toward the middle of the tester **(fig. 4)**.

7. As the stick gets closer to the middle, notice when you can see movement, shape, and color of the letter or number **(fig. 5)**. Record the degree that you can see movement, shape, and color.

8. Repeat the test several times on both sides of your head.

Fig. 2: Label the tester.

Fig. 3: Write a number on a craft stick.

Fig. 4: Move the stick around the tester.

Fig. 5: Note where you can see movement, shape, and color.

THINKING DEEPER

Cone receptors are used to see color and for sharp vision, but they need bright light to work. Use the tester while you change the brightness of a room to see where an image comes into focus and where you can see color. Also change the images on your craft stick. For example, attach pictures of different animals to the stick to see when you can identify them. You might not be able to distinguish between a dog and a cat until the image is right in front of you.

WHAT'S GOING ON?

As the image on the craft stick is moved, light reflected from the stick enters your eye through your cornea and pupil. After moving through the lens of your eye, the light falls on photoreceptors in your retina. Light coming from the right side falls on the left side of your retinas and light from the left side falls on the right side of your retinas. As the stick is moved toward the center of the tester, light from the image falls on more central parts of your retina.

You likely were able to see movement when the stick was out to the side of your head, but could not see colors or shapes until the stick made its way to the middle of the tester. You might not have been able to see clearly until the stick was at the very middle of the tester. This lab shows that the photoreceptors responsible for seeing movement, shape, and color are located in different parts of your retina.

Cone receptors are responsible for color vision and are located primarily in the central part of the retina. Rod receptors are found in high numbers along the sides of the retina and do not provide information about color, but they are sensitive to movement.

BRAIN FACTS

→ Some animals have photoreceptors that allow them to see ultraviolet or infrared radiation.

→ The box jellyfish has twenty-four eyes.

When does red become green and blue become yellow? Right here in this lab.

Fig. 3: Stare at them for 15 seconds.

⏰ Time

→ 10 minutes

Materials

→ Red, blue, green, and yellow markers.
→ White paper

✏️ Method

1. Using red, yellow, green, and blue markers **(fig. 1)**, draw four squares **(fig. 2)** that are 1¼ by 1¼ inches (3 by 3 cm)

2. Stare at the center of your squares for 15 seconds **(fig. 3)**.

Fig. 1: Use red, yellow, green, and blue markers.

Fig. 2: Make four squares.

Fig. 4: Then stare at blank white paper to see the afterimage.

3. Move your gaze to the middle of a blank area of your paper **(fig. 4)**.

4. Notice the colors and their locations on the paper.

WHAT'S GOING ON?

The retinas of your eyes have different types of cells that respond to different wavelengths of light. Cells called cones are most sensitive to red, blue, or green light. When you stare at a particular color for too long, these receptors get tired. When you then look at the white background, the receptors that are tired do not work as well. Therefore, the information from all of the different color receptors is not in balance and you see color "afterimages." After a short time, the receptors are ready to work again and your vision quickly returns to normal.

THINKING DEEPER

Digital photographs can be used to create some unusual color afterimages. Find a brightly colored photograph on a computer. Hold a piece of white paper near the computer screen. After you stare at the photograph for about 15 seconds, shift your gaze to the white paper to see an afterimage.

BENHAM'S DISKS

BRAIN FACTS

→ The announce-ment of Benham's disk was published in 1894 in the jour-nal *Nature* with the title "Artificial Spectrum Top."[3]

→ Scientists Gustav Fechner and Hermann von Helmholtz experimented with black-and-white disks before Mr. Benham did. Fechner and von Helmholtz both noticed that spinning these disks produced the perception of colors.

[3] Vol. 51, pp. 113–114.

Make colors appear by spinning a black-and-white disk.

Fig. 1: Paint a CD half black and half white.

⏰ Time
→ 1 hour

🚀 Materials
→ White and black paint
→ Paintbrushes
→ Compact disk
→ Black marker
→ Glue
→ Marble

✏️ Method
1. Paint half of the compact disk black and the other half white **(fig. 1)**.

(continued next page)

WHAT'S GOING ON?

In 1894, toymaker C. E. Benham discovered that a spinning disk with a particular pattern of black-and-white marks could cause people to see colors. Mr. Benham called his disk an Artificial Spectrum Top and sold it through Messrs. Newton and Co. Benham's top (or Benham's disk) has puzzled scientists for more than 100 years.

The retina of the eye is composed of two types of receptors sensitive to light: cones and rods. Cones are important for color vision and for seeing in bright light. There are three types of cones, each of which is most sensitive to a particular wavelength of light. Rods are important for seeing in low light.

The colors that appear in spinning Benham's disks may be the result of changes that occur in the retina and other parts of the visual system. The black-and-white areas of the disk may activate neighboring areas of the retina differently. This alternating response may cause an interaction within the nervous system that generates colors.

Another theory for the perception of Benham disk colors concerns how different types of cones require different times to respond and the fact that they stay activated for different amounts of time. Therefore, when you spin a disk, the white color activates all three types of cones, but then the black deactivates them. The activation/deactivation sequence causes an imbalance in the signaling because the different types of cones take different times to respond and stay on for different lengths of time. This imbalance of information received by the brain results in the perception of color. Neither of these theories explains Benham disk colors completely and the reason behind the illusion remains unsolved.

BENHAM'S DISKS (continued)

BRAIN FACTS

→ The colors that you see when you spin Benham's disks have been called "subjective colors," "Fechner-Benham colors," "Prevost-Fechner-Benham colors," "polyphan colors," and "pattern-induced flicker colors" (PIFCs).

Fig. 2: Draw patterned lines on the white surface.

2. After the paint is dry, use a black marker **(fig. 2)** to draw a pattern of lines on the white side of the compact disk (see sample patterns).

3. Turn the disk over so the unpainted side is facing up. Glue a marble in the middle hole of the disk **(fig. 3)**. Let the glue dry.

4. To spin the disk, place the marble on the table, press down lightly on the disk, and give it a twist **(fig. 4)**. What colors do you see?

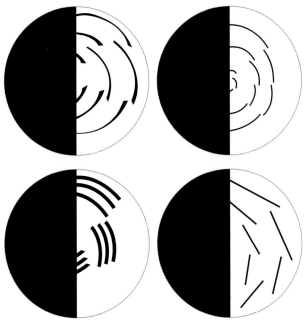

Sample Patterns

Fig. 3: Glue a marble to the bottom of the CD.

Fig. 4: Give it a spin.

THINKING DEEPER

Some people notice that Benham disk colors change with the speed of the spinning disk. Experiment with different spinning speeds and with the spin direction (clockwise, counterclockwise) to determine when colors appear and when they are brightest. Also, experiment with different lighting conditions. Try the disks in sunlight, under incandescent lightbulbs, and under fluorescent lights to see whether there are any differences in the perceptions of color.

The patterns used for the Benham's disks in this experiment are only samples. Continue your investigation by changing the amount of the disk that is colored black and white. Also, change the thickness of the black lines, the number of black lines, the location of black lines, and the pattern of black lines. Note how these changes alter the perception of color with you spin a disk. You can even change the color of the lines. What happens when you use blue instead of black lines?

Additional clues about the how the disks work may be revealed by asking people who are color blind what they see in Benham's disks. People who are color blind are missing one or more cone receptors in their retinas. Ask these people what they see when they look at a spinning Benham disk and compare their perceptions to people who are not color blind.

UNIT 07

TOUCH

YOUR SENSE OF TOUCH makes it easy for you to know whether, for instance, you are petting the soft fur of a cat or tapping the sharp end of a pin. Below the first layer of skin, the epidermis, is the dermis, which contains receptors that allow you to respond to touch. Touch is actually a group of several senses rather than just one. Attached to the receptors are neurons, which send signals not only about touch, but also about pain, heat, cold, and pressure to your nervous system. Different receptors inside the skin make it possible for you to know about the pressure, vibration, stretching, and texture of an object.

Using your sense of touch, you also know what part of your body is touching an object and if the object is moving. Even a light touch activates your sensory receptors. The receptors are connected to axons, which send electrical signals to the spinal cord. The brain receives that information and you're able to tell where another person/object is making contact with your skin as well as what the person/object feels like. The labs in this section explore the sensitivity of your skin and the perceptions that result from the objects that touch your skin.

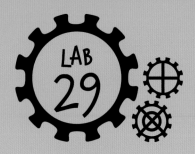

ONE POINT, TWO POINT

BRAIN FACTS

→ Skin without any hair is called glabrous skin.

→ Different types of skin receptors respond to different types of touch. Ruffini nerve endings are receptors that respond to pressure, Meissner corpuscles respond to light touch, Pacinian corpuscles respond to vibration, and free nerve endings respond to temperature and pain.

→ Adult humans have about 9 pounds (4.1 kg) of skin—the largest organ of the body.

What area of your body is most sensitive to touch?

⏰ Time
→ 45 minutes

Materials
→ Toothpicks
→ Ruler
→ Rubber bands

⚠ Safety Tips
→ Be extremely careful if you test skin on the face. Remember to use only a light touch and do not get the toothpick close to your test subject's eyes.

Method

1. Secure two toothpicks to a ruler with rubber bands **(fig. 1)**. One should be lined up with the first mark at the beginning of the ruler; the other should be placed about 1¼ inches (3 cm) away from the other toothpick. Make sure that the tips of the toothpicks are even with each other.

2. Lightly touch the ends of the toothpicks to the back of the hand

Fig. 3: Make sure both tips touch the skin at the same time.

of your subject **(fig. 2)**. Your subject should not look at the area of skin that is being tested. Do not press too hard.

3. Make sure both tips touch the skin at the same time. Ask your subject whether he or she feels one or two pressure points **(fig. 3)**. If your subject says one point, then spread the toothpicks a bit further apart, and touch the back of the hand again. If your subject reports two points, then push the tips a bit closer together, and test again.

4. Read the distance on the ruler between the points that the subject reports a change from "I feel two points" to "I feel one point" **(fig. 4)**.

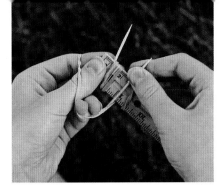
Fig. 1: Secure a toothpick to a ruler.

Fig. 2: Lightly touch subject's hand with toothpicks.

Fig. 4: Measure the distance.

THINKING DEEPER

Use the one point–two point test to investigate the sensitivity of touch in other parts of the body, such as the arms, legs, fingers, back, neck, head, palms, and toes. Compare the distances required for the response on different body regions and see how they match with the results of a published experiment (see table below).[4] Which part of the body is most sensitive? In other words, which part of the body had the smallest distance where two toothpick points could be detected?

SITE	THRESHOLD DISTANCE	SITE	THRESHOLD DISTANCE
Fingers	0.8 to 0.12 inch (2 to 3 mm)	Upper lip	0.20 inch (5 mm)
Cheek	0.24 inch (6 mm)	Nose	0.28 inch (7 mm)
Palm	0.41 inch (10 mm)	Forehead	0.61 inch (15 mm)
Foot	0.82 inch (20 mm)	Belly	1.22 inches (30 mm)
Forearm	1.43 inches (35 mm)	Upper arm	1.59 inches (39 mm)
Back	1.59 inches (39 mm)	Shoulder	1.67 inches (41 mm)
Thigh	1.71 inches (42 mm)	Calf	1.84 inches (45 mm)

[4] These data (rounded) are from a threshold experiment published in *The Skin Senses*, edited by D. R. Kenshalo (Springfield, IL: Thomas, 1968).

WHAT'S GOING ON?

Skin is made of several layers. The outermost layer of skin is called the epidermis. The epidermis makes new skin cells, gives skin its color, and helps protect the body. Below the epidermis is the dermis. In addition to making sweat and oil, growing hair, and providing blood to the skin, the dermis contains special cells (receptors) that respond to touch. Skin receptors are attached to neurons that send signals into the nervous system about touch, temperature, pressure, and pain.

The receptors in our skin are not distributed in an even way around our bodies. The skin in some places, such as our fingers and lips, has more touch receptors than the skin in other parts of our body, such as our backs and legs.

MAKE YOUR POINT

BRAIN FACTS

→ Pressure can be detected when the skin on some parts of the body is moved only 0.001 mm.

→ The star-nosed mole has almost six times more touch receptors in its nose than humans have in their hands.

→ Somatosensation refers to sensory information about the skin.

Become a neurologist! Make your own set of touch testers to measure someone's ability to detect pressure.

⏰ Time

→ 30 minutes

🔑 Materials

→ Scissors
→ Monofilament fishing line in several thicknesses
→ Ruler
→ Glue
→ Craft sticks
→ Blindfold

📝 Method

1. Use scissors to cut various thick-nesses of monofilament fishing line into 1½-inch (4 cm) lengths **(fig. 1)**.

2. Glue each piece of fishing line at a right angle to the end of a craft stick to make a tester **(fig. 2)**. Let the glue dry **(fig. 3)**. Your completed testing apparatus (tester) should look like this:

Fig. 1: Cut fishing line into 1½-inch (4 cm) lengths.

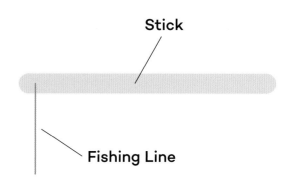

Stick

Fishing Line

Fig. 2: Glue fishing line to sticks at right angles.

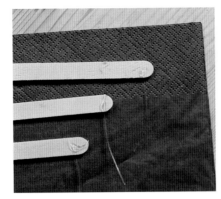

Fig. 3: Let glue dry.

Fig. 4: Touch line to subject's hand.

3. To measure the sensitivity of your test subjects, blindfold them. Touch the tester to the skin on the hands of your test subjects until the fishing line bends **(fig. 4)**.

4. Ask your test subjects whether they felt anything.

5. If your subject does not feel anything, use a thicker line and repeat the test. If your subject does feel the touch, use a thinner line and repeat the test.

6. Record the size of the thinnest fishing line that your test subjects could feel.

WHAT'S GOING ON?

The tactile detection threshold is the smallest amount of touch necessary for someone to say, "Hey, I feel that." The different thicknesses of fishing line allow you to vary the amount of pressure applied to the skin on different parts of the body. A person can feel the touch when enough signals from skin receptors reach the brain.

THINKING DEEPER

Use the touch testers on different parts of your test subject's body. Compare the detection threshold for the skin on the fingers, hands, arms, back, legs, and feet. What is the most sensitive and least sensitive area of the body? Also compare the detection thresholds for young people and old people and for boys and girls.

SANDPAPER TESTERS

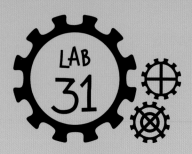

BRAIN FACTS

→ The eyelids have the thinnest skin on your body.

→ Some people are born without the ability to sense pain.

Demonstrate the exquisite sensitivity of the sense of touch with sandpaper.

⏰ Time

→ 30 minutes

🔑 Materials

→ **Sandpaper in 5 different grit sizes**
→ **Scissors**
→ **Cardboard**
→ **Glue**

📝 Method

1. Get five different grits (roughness) of sandpaper. The degree of roughness should be printed on the back of the sandpaper sheet.

2. Cut the sandpaper into pieces about 4 by 4 inches (10 by 10 cm) so you have five pieces of each grade of sandpaper.

3. Cut twenty-five pieces of cardboard into 4 by 4-inch (10 by 10 cm) squares **(fig. 1)**.

4. Glue each piece of sandpaper to a piece of cardboard.

5. Write the grade of roughness on the rough side (sandpaper side) on each sandpaper/cardboard piece.

6. Mix the pieces of sandpaper and place them with the rough side down **(fig. 2)**.

7. Rub your finger on the sandpaper to feel the grit.

Fig. 1: Cut sandpaper.

Fig. 2: Mix the pieces rough side down.

Fig. 3: Sort sandpaper into piles by feel.

8. Based on your feeling of the sandpaper, make five piles of five cards, each with a single grit of sandpaper **(fig. 3)**.

9. Order the piles from the smoothest to the roughest.

10. Flip over the cards and see whether you placed the same sandpaper grits in the same piles.

WHAT'S GOING ON?

Rubbing your finger over the sandpaper stimulates receptors in your skin such as Pacinian corpuscles and Meissner corpuscles. As each bump in the sandpaper moves over a receptor, a signal is generated. The skin receptors connect to axons in nerves that send electrical signals into the spinal cord. From the spinal cord, the signals make their way to the brain for the perception of touch and roughness.

THINKING DEEPER

Try the sandpaper test again, but this time, press your finger on the sandpaper rather than rubbing your finger on the sandpaper. Compare the sensation of the sandpaper press to the sensation you felt when you rubbed the sandpaper. Also, check the accuracy of your sandpaper piles with this new method.

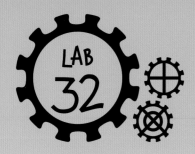

LAB 32

BRAILLE ALPHABET

BRAIN FACTS

→ Louis Braille, who was born in France on January 4, 1809, developed the system of raised dots for people who are blind when he was only fifteen years old. Braille lost his eyesight in a workshop accident when he was a young child.

→ The average reading speed of Braille is about 125 words per minute.

Make your own Braille alphabet to test your sensitivity to touch.

⏱ Time

→ 30 minutes

🔧 Materials

→ **Braille alphabet sheet**
→ **Paper**
→ **White glue**
→ **Scissors**

📝 Method

1. Each letter in the Braille alphabet uses a series of black dots. Photocopy the image or print one out from a computer **(fig. 1)**.

2. Place small dots of white glue on the location of each black dot **(fig. 2)**.

3. Separate each letter by a small space **(fig. 3)**.

4. When the glue dries, you will have created Braille letters that you can feel.

5. Cut out each letter and try to arrange the letters in alphabetical order using only your sense of touch.

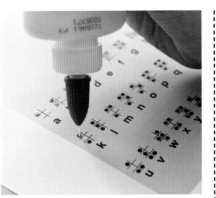

Fig. 1: Each Braille letter uses a series of dots.

Fig. 2: Place small dots of glue on each black dot.

Fig. 3: Separate letters by a small space.

WHAT'S GOING ON?

Braille symbols use a system of raised dots that can be read by the sense of touch. People who are blind or have low vision move their fingers over the dots to feel different letters. By understanding the meaning of the dots, people can read words.

THINKING DEEPER

Teach yourself to read Braille. First, learn A through J because these use only the top four dots. The next ten letters (K through T) are similar to the first ten letters except they use one more dot in the lower left. The letters U, V, X, Y, and Z are similar to K, L, M, N, and O except they have another dot in the lower right. The letter W does not follow the other letter pattern. Practice recognizing the different letters using only your sense of touch. Put letters together to spell words. When you are ready, go to your local library and ask a librarian for a book printed with Braille. Can you read the book?

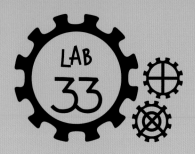

LAB 33

TOUCH HERE, TOUCH THERE

BRAIN FACTS

→ A protein called melanin is responsible for the color of skin.

→ Everyone should wear sunscreen to protect the skin from the damaging effects of the Sun.

→ The brain makes chemicals called endorphins that act on neurons and reduce pain.

Test your accuracy to find a spot touched on your skin.

⏰ Time
→ 30 minutes

Materials
→ Blindfold
→ Washable markers in 2 different colors
→ Ruler

Method

1. Blindfold your test subject. Touch a spot on the arm of the subject with one marker, leaving a small mark **(fig. 1)**.

2. Give your blindfolded test subject a marker with a different color **(fig. 2)**.

3. Ask your test subject to use the marker to touch the point that you just touched **(fig. 3)**.

Fig. 1: Blindfold a test subject and touch spot on arm with a marker.

4. Using the ruler, measure the distance from your point to the point touched by your subject **(fig. 4)**.

5. Repeat this test several times on different parts of your test subject's arm and hand.

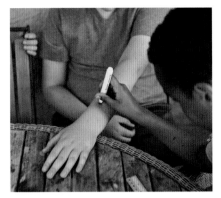

Fig. 2: Give person a second mark with a different color.

Fig. 3: Ask subject to touch the point.

Fig. 4: Use a ruler to see how close they were.

WHAT'S GOING ON?

A light touch to the skin activates sensory receptors. These receptors are connected to axons that send electrical signals to the spinal cord. Information then travels to the brain and allows a person to know what and where something touched the skin. Areas of skin with small distances between the two marked spots indicate more sensitive areas of the body. Areas that are more sensitive to touch have more receptors.

THINKING DEEPER

In addition to testing the skin on the hands and arms, test other parts of the body, such as the feet, legs, and torso. Compare the distances to identify the part of the body that has the smallest distance between the two spots. To make the test more difficult, ask your test subjects to touch the marked spot on the opposite side of their body. In other words, if you touch the middle part of your subjects' left hand, ask them to mark the identical spot on their right hand. To make the test even more difficult, have your test subjects wait a minute or two after you mark a spot before they mark their spot.

THE LITTLE BOX OF SCIENCE

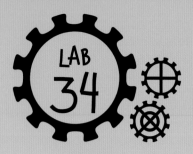

BRAIN FACTS

→ The total surface area of the skin is about 3,000 square inches (1.93 m²).

→ There are approximately 17,000 touch receptors in the hand.

→ People report pain when temperatures reach 113°F (45°C).

What could it be? Only the Little Box of Science knows for sure.

⏰ Time

→ 1 hour

🪶 Materials

→ Scissors
→ Shoe box
→ Sock
→ Tape (duct tape is best)
→ Decorations for the box, such as drawings, photos, and stickers
→ Objects to put in the box

📝 Method

1. With scissors, cut a hole in the side of a box that is large enough for your hand (**fig. 1**).

2. Cut off the toe end of the sock to make a tube.

3. Tape one end of the sock to the inside of the box so that the sock makes a "tunnel" from the outside to the inside of the box (**fig. 2**).

Fig. 1: Cut a hole larger than your hand in a box.

4. Decorate the box with pictures, photos, and stickers.

5. Place several small objects into the box (**fig. 3**).

6. Ask your test subjects to reach into the box through the sock to identify the objects (**fig. 4**).

Fig. 2: Cut a sock and tape it to the box.

Fig. 3: Place objects in the box.

Fig. 4: Try to identify them by touch.

WHAT'S GOING ON?

You can make this lab easy by using common, familiar objects, such as a spoon, a small ball, or a sponge. To make the lab more difficult, use unusual items, such as a bar of soap, piece of foil, or toy animal. Also, add wooden or plastic letters or numbers to the box and try to identify them. The box could be used in a match game if you have pairs of objects. One object goes into the box while its matching pair is shown or placed in the hand of your test subject. Your test subject must then reach into the box to find the matching item.

Wear a pair of gloves to understand the importance of your skin and its receptors to your ability to feel. Rubber dishwashing gloves, cotton gloves, or leather gloves will prevent many of the receptors in your skin from responding when you reach into the box.

THINKING DEEPER

The box is used to isolate the sense of touch from sight and hearing. Therefore, touch is the main sense that can be used to identify the object. However, we have other senses that help with this function. For example, we have special sensory cells in our joints and muscles that tell us about body position and muscle strength. The weight of an object might give a clue about its identity.

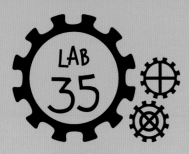

LAB 35

TOUCH MAZE

BRAIN FACTS

→ Sensory information from receptors in the skin is processed in the parietal lobe of the brain in the somatosensory cortex.

→ The Pacinian corpuscle receptor was named after Italian anatomist Filippo Pacini (1812–1883).

If you think mazes are difficult to navigate when you can see, try to complete one using only your sense of touch.

Fig. 2: Navigate the maze.

⏰ Time
→ 30 minutes

✏️ Materials
→ Scissors
→ Piece of cardboard at least 6 by 6 inches (21 by 21 cm)
→ Pencil
→ White glue

📝 Method

1. With scissors, cut out squares of cardboard. Each square should be about 6 by 6 inches (21x21 cm).

2. Draw a trail maze on the cardboard with a pencil.

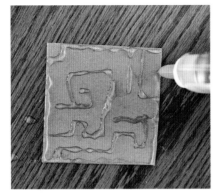

Fig. 1: Apply glue in maze shape.

Fig. 3: Apply more glue to make ridges higher.

Fig. 4: Try again.

3. Apply a layer of glue over the trail **(fig. 1)**.

4. After the glue is dry, close your eyes and navigate the maze by holding your finger on the glue trail **(fig. 2)**.

THINKING DEEPER

If your maze is too difficult to follow, let the glue dry and then apply another layer of glue to raise the height of the maze **(fig. 3)**. This should make it easier for you to follow the path **(fig. 4)**. In fact, you could make several mazes with the same path but different heights. Use a timer to see whether there are any differences in the time it takes to navigate through the different mazes. You can also use one maze to investigate the effects of learning. Start a timer at the same time you start to move through a maze. When you finish a maze, record the amount of time it took you to finish. Repeat your journey through the same maze several times and record your times. Make a graph with the trial number on the x-axis and your time on the y-axis to see whether you improved over time.

WHAT'S GOING ON?

As you move your finger over the glue, touch receptors send information to the spinal cord and up to the brain. If your brain detects that your finger is no longer on the glue trail, signals are sent back down to your spinal cord and then out to muscles in your arms, hands, and fingers to correct your error. This pathway from the skin on your finger to the brain and then from the brain back to the finger helps you navigate the maze.

UNIT 08

HEARING

THOSE FLOPPY THINGS on the sides of your head are not just for show. Your ears help you identify and respond to what is happening in the environment around you. Noises—everything from fire engine sirens and barking dogs to ocean waves and windswept leaves—create sound waves, which are invisible vibrations in the air. This vibration causes changes in air pressure that move the eardrum, or the tympanic membrane, inside your ear. There are three small bones called the malleus, incus, and stapes that are connected to the eardrum. These bones receive these vibrations from the eardrum due to their close proximity to it. The bones send the vibrations to the cochlea, a snail-shaped structure inside the ear. The receptor cells in the cochlea create electrical signals that travel from the ear to the brain.

Your brain creates the perception of sound to help you understand the loudness and pitch of a noise. Your brain uses these perceptions to help you identify voices, avoid danger, communicate with others, and enjoy music. The labs in this section investigate the nature of sound, illustrate how changes in air pressure create the perception of sound, and introduce the roles your brain, cochlear receptors, and auditory nerve play in receiving and processing sound.

EARDRUM MODEL

BRAIN FACTS

→ A frog's eardrum is located outside its body behind its eye.

→ People can hear sound waves with frequencies between 20 and 20,000 hertz (Hz).

→ The smallest bone in the human body is one of the bones in the ear called the stapes. The stapes is 0.10 to 0.13 inch (2.5 to 3.3 mm) long and weighs 1.9 to 4.3 milligrams.

Make a simple model of the eardrum (tympanic membrane) to see how sound travels through the air and vibrates the eardrum.

⏰ Time

→ **20 minutes**

🪝 Materials

→ **Plastic wrap**
→ **Container with wide opening**
→ **Rubber band**
→ **Uncooked rice or other small grain**
→ **Metal cookie sheet (or other noise maker)**

📝 Method

1. Stretch a piece of plastic wrap over a large container. Make sure the plastic wrap is stretched tightly **(fig. 1)**.

2. Use a rubber band to secure the plastic wrap over the top of the container **(fig. 2)**.

Fig. 1: Stretch plastic over open container.

3. Place a few grains of uncooked rice on top of the plastic wrap **(fig. 3)**.

4. Hold the cookie sheet close to the plastic wrap.

5. Hit the cookie sheet to create a loud noise and see if the rice grains move **(fig. 4)**.

Fig. 2: Secure with rubber band.

Fig. 3: Place rice on plastic and bang cookie sheet.

Fig. 4: Watch the rice grains move from the sound vibrations.

THINKING DEEPER

Most musical instruments create sound by causing some kind of vibration. For example, guitars and violins have strings that vibrate at different frequencies. The different lengths, thicknesses, tension, and materials of the strings change the sound. Sounds from trumpets and clarinets are created when a column of air vibrates.

Make a simple musical instrument with a plastic or wooden ruler. Hold the ruler flat on a table so that most of the ruler is hanging over the edge. Use your free hand to bend the part of the ruler over the edge and then quickly release it. The ruler should bounce up and down and create a sound. Experiment by strumming different lengths of the ruler hanging over the edge. Compare the sounds the ruler makes with the frequency of the bouncing ruler.

WHAT'S GOING ON?

The "big bang" produces sound waves (changes in air pressure) that cause the plastic sheet to vibrate. The vibration of the plastic sheet causes the rice grains to move. Sound waves vibrate the eardrum (tympanic membrane) in much the same way. The eardrum is connected to three small bones (malleus, incus, and stapes) in the ear. Therefore, when the eardrum vibrates, the bones also vibrate. The bones pass the vibrations to a snail-shaped, fluid-filled structure in the inner ear called the cochlea. The cochlea has receptor cells that generate electrical signals that are sent to the brain through the auditory nerve.

SOUND SHAKERS

BRAIN FACTS

→ Exposure to loud sounds can damage receptor cells in the cochlea and cause hearing loss.

→ Elephants can hear sounds made by other elephants 6.2 miles (10 km) away.

Make some noise! Explore hearing with these easy-to-make sound shakers.

⏰ Time

→ 30 minutes

🖌 Materials

→ Plastic containers with covers or tops, such as film canisters, yogurt cups, or plastic bottles
→ Filling such as dry seeds, uncooked beans or rice, sand, pebbles, coins, marbles, and rocks
→ Tape
→ Decorations such as stickers, colored papers, and cutouts from magazines (optional)

✏️ Method

1. Fill different containers one-quarter or half full with dry seeds, uncooked beans or rice, pebbles, sand, or other small objects **(fig. 1)**.

Fig. 1: Fill containers.

2. Seal the top of the containers with a lid or tape to prevent the filling from falling out **(fig. 2)**.

3. Optional: Decorate the container with stickers, colored paper, or magazine cutouts.

4. Shake the containers **(fig. 3)** and compare the sounds made by the different materials **(fig. 4)**.

Fig. 2: Seal top and decorate.

Fig. 3: Shake and compare sounds.

Fig. 4: Do different material sound different?

WHAT'S GOING ON?

Sound waves made by these shakers cause changes in air pressure. When the sound waves enter the ear, they vibrate the eardrum. The vibrations of the eardrum move three interconnected bones in the middle ear. The bones move fluid contained in a spiral-shaped structure called the cochlea. Inside the cochlea is a membrane that has receptor cells that send electrical signals when they move. These electrical signals travel to the brain through the auditory nerve. Sounds are perceived when the signals arrive at the auditory cortex in the temporal lobe of the brain.

THINKING DEEPER

Use the sound shakers to play a guessing game. Can other people guess what you put inside each container? You can also create two sound shakers with the same materials to see whether people can find matching sounds. If you make similar sound shakers, ensure that the same amount of material is placed inside each container so people cannot use the weight of the shaker to find the matching pairs.

BRAIN FACTS

→ A dog whistle makes a high-frequency sound that dogs (and cats) can hear, but humans cannot hear.

→ The speed of sound in air is approximately 767.4 miles (1,235 km) per hour.

Now it's time to go outside and take a walk. Don't forget your lab notebook.

Fig. 5: Do you hear the same things?

 Time
→ 30 minutes

Materials
→ Paper
→ Pen or pencil

Method

1. Find a nice place to have a walk, such as a park, the beach, or the mall **(fig. 1)**.

2. Now listen **(fig. 2)**.

3. Write down all of the sounds that you hear **(fig. 3)**.

Fig. 1: Find a nice place to have a seat

Fig. 2: Listen.

Fig. 3: Write down what you hear.

Fig. 4: Compare the sounds that everyone heard.

WHAT'S GOING ON?

The sounds that we normally hear are only a small fraction of the sounds in our environment. It is impossible for us to pay attention to everything that is happening around us. Much of what happens in the environment is not important to us, so we ignore it. In this lab, you were required to pay attention to sounds that you would likely not hear.

When something happens that is important to us, even though we are not paying attention to it, we become aware of it. For example, if you are having lunch in a noisy place and talking to some friends, if someone at another table says your name, you will likely hear it even though you were not part of the conversation at the other table.

THINKING DEEPER

Send some friends on a walk to record the sounds they hear. They can go out by themselves or in groups. Tell everyone to write down everything that they hear within a specific amount of time. In addition, everyone must stay within a certain area, such as a park, playground, or backyard. When the time is up, compare sound lists **(fig. 4)** to see whether everyone heard the same things **(fig. 5)**.

BRAIN FACTS

→ Dolphins and bats send out sound waves and then wait for the signals to bounce back to them. This is called echolocation. These animals use echolocation to find food and move through their environment.

→ The loudness of sound is measured in decibels.

How important is it to have two ears? Compare the ability to judge distance using one and two ears.

Fig. 2: Measure distance and mark.

⏰ Time

→ 30 minutes

🦜 Materials

→ Tape
→ Yardstick or tape measure
→ A noisemaker, such as a bell
→ Marker

📝 Method

1. Make an X on the floor with tape **(fig. 1)**.

2. Measure distances in increments of 6 feet (2 m) from the X and place a strip of tape at each point **(fig. 2)**.

3. Label each distance from the X with a marker: 6, 12, 18, 24 feet, etc. (2, 4, 6, 8 m, etc.).

4. Have your test subject stand on the X with his or her eyes closed.

5. You should stand on one of the tape marks facing your subject **(fig. 3)**.

6. Ring the bell. Your test subject must now tell you which line you are standing on.

7. Try different distances and record whether your test subject was able to judge each distance correctly **(fig. 4)**.

8. Repeat the experiment, but this time have your test subject cover one ear with his or her hand.

Fig. 1: Make an X with tape.

Fig. 3: Stand on marks and ring the bell.

Fig. 4: Try it with more than one person at different distances!

WHAT'S GOING ON?

Most people will find that it is easier to locate sounds when they use two ears. The ability to judge the location of sounds is influenced by two factors. First, sound coming from one side of the body has a direct path to the ear on that side, but the head blocks the sound to the ear on the other side. Therefore, sound coming into the ear on the same side as the source of the sound is a little louder than the sound coming into the ear on the opposite side. Second, there is a small difference between the times when sound enters each ear. The brain is able to use this time difference to help locate sounds. When one ear is closed, the brain cannot use the differences in the loudness of sound from each ear or the differences in the time it takes sounds to reach each ear. Therefore, it is harder to locate sound when one ear is blocked.

THINKING DEEPER

Investigate the factors involved with sound localization by changing how your test subjects listen to sound. Ask your test subjects to face away from you or turn to one side when they try to identify the location of sound. Now check the accuracy of identifying the location of sound with one and two ears.

UNIT 09

SLEEP AND BODY RHYTHMS

WE SPEND ABOUT ONE-THIRD of our lives asleep, unaware of our surroundings. Wouldn't it be great if we did not have to sleep? We could get so much more done. However, sleep is critical to our well-being. Without a good night's sleep, we feel anxious and tired and have problems making good decisions.

Your body and brain have a built-in clock that works on a 24-hour cycle. During a 24-hour period, different body systems move from being active to being less active. Attention, heart rate, body temperature, and hormone levels are just a few of the many functions that follow daily rhythms.

The labs in this section will allow you to explore the ups and downs of biological rhythms in yourself, in other people, and in animals. The methods and materials used in these labs are simple, but they all require that you make careful observations. While you study yourself, record your behavior in as much detail as possible. Study others in their natural environments, but do not disturb them or influence them in any way.

SLEEP LOG

→ Humans sleep about 8 hours each day. Giraffes sleep only about 2 hours a day and brown bats sleep about 20 hours a day.

→ Insomnia is a common sleep disorder.

→ Benjamin Franklin wrote, "Early to bed, and early to rise, makes a man healthy, wealthy and wise."[5]

A sleep log is a great way to study sleep by keeping a record of your sleep behavior and the dreams that you have each night.

Time

→ A few minutes each day for at least 1 week

Materials

→ Pen or pencil
→ Lab notebook

Method

1. Keep a pen and your lab notebook near your bed **(fig. 1)**.

2. Go to sleep **(fig. 2)**.

3. When you wake up, immediately write down or record everything that you remember about your dreams.

[5] *Poor Richard's Almanack*, 1758.

Fig. 1: Keep a pen and lab notebook near your bed.

Fig. 2: Go to sleep.

WHAT'S GOING ON?

It is best to write down your dreams immediately after you wake up because the events and details of dreams will fade with time. After a few nights of practice recording your dreams, you should get better at remembering what happened while you were dreaming.

While you sleep, your brain cycles through a regular pattern of electrical activity. Remember, neurons are like little batteries that generate small amounts of electricity. Sleep researchers can record this electrical brain activity (brain waves) by attaching electrodes to the scalp of a person. A machine called an electroencephalograph (EEG) can amplify and record the electrical signals.

When a person is awake, the EEG pattern has a small size with very frequent waves. After a person falls asleep, the EEG pattern slows down and the size of the waves increases. The EEG pattern then cycles back to a smaller size with waves that are more frequent. About 90 minutes after a person falls asleep, the EEG pattern looks as if a person is awake. However, if you looked at the muscle activity in this sleeping person, it would appear as if the person was paralyzed. This stage of sleep is called paradoxical sleep because the EEG pattern looks as if the person is awake. Because the muscles of the person are paralyzed, a person cannot move during paradoxical sleep. Most dreaming occurs during paradoxical sleep, also known as rapid eye movement (REM) sleep because this is a time when a sleeper's eyes move back and forth.

THINKING DEEPER

Try to remember whether your dreams were in color and write down as many details as possible. You should even record your emotions, the places you visited, and the names of people in your dreams. Look back at your dream record to see whether something happened while you were awake that ended up in your dream.

You might want to investigate factors that affect your dreams. For example, compare the content of your dreams when you go to sleep in a good mood and when you are stressed and anxious. The time you go to sleep and the season may also affect your dreams, so do not forget to record what time you turn out the lights, the day of the week, and the date. After you have collected many dream records, go back to your log and look for trends in the amount of sleep you had and the details of your dreams.

Sleep and Body Rhythms **111**

REM DETECTIVE

BRAIN FACTS

→ Dreaming can happen outside of REM sleep, but the most intense dreams occur during REM sleep.

→ Newborn babies can sleep up to 16 hours a day and spend about half of their time sleeping in REM sleep.

→ Dolphins, whales, and some birds sleep with one side of their brains at a time.

Observe a sleeping person to detect when he or she is in rapid eye movement (REM) sleep.

Fig. 1: Practice observing eye movement.

Fig. 2: See what happens when closed eyes move from side to side.

Fig. 3: When your test subject is asleep, observe his or her eye movements.

⏰ Time

→ 30 minutes

🪁 Materials

→ A sleeping subject, such as a family member or friend

🔺 Safety Tips

→ Be quiet and do not to wake up the person (or animal) you are observing.

📝 Method

1. Practice observing eye movements by asking your test subjects to close their eyes **(fig. 1)**.

2. Then ask them to move their eyes from side to side **(fig. 2)**.

3. Notice a small bulge moving behind your subject's eyelids.

4. When your test subject is asleep, observe his or her eye movements **(fig. 3)**.

❓ WHAT'S GOING ON?

Rapid eye movement (REM) sleep is the stage of sleep when most dreaming occurs. Sleep researchers use expensive electronic equipment to monitor brain waves to detect REM sleep, but this lab uses just your power of observation. When people enter REM sleep, their eyes move back and forth. You should be able to see this eye movement, even when your test subject's eyes are closed. You must be patient because it could take 90 minutes for a person to enter REM sleep after they fall asleep. Also, a REM period lasts only a few minutes.

THINKING DEEPER

All animals show signs of rest or sleep. Observe how a pet or an animal at the zoo sleeps. You might notice an animal's eyes move during REM periods or muscle movements during other stages of sleep.

BRAIN FACTS

→ Sleepwalking does not occur during REM sleep; people do not act out dreams while they sleepwalk.

→ Narcolepsy is a sleep disorder in which REM sleep suddenly starts when someone is awake.

How long does it take you to fall asleep? Sleep researcher Dr. William C. Dement suggests this easy way to measure the time it takes you to fall asleep.[6]

⏰ Time

→ **30 minutes**

🖌 Materials

→ **Large dinner plate**
→ **Lab notebook**
→ **Pencil or pen**
→ **Clock (or timer)**
→ **Metal spoon**

📝 Method

1. Place the plate on the floor near the side of your bed.

2. In your notebook, write down the time you get into bed.

3. Get into bed and hold a metal spoon in one hand over the plate on the floor **(fig. 1)**.

Fig. 1: Go to bed holding a spoon over a plate on the floor.

4. Fall asleep **(fig. 2)**.

5. If you wake up to the sound of the spoon hitting the place, note the time in your notebook **(fig. 3)**.

6. Repeat the experiment holding the spoon over the plate or just go back to sleep.

[6] W. C. Dement and C. C. Vaughn, *The Promise of Sleep: A Pioneer in Sleep Medicine Explores the Vital Connection Between Health, Happiness, and a Good Night's Sleep* (New York: Delacorte Press, 1999).

Fig. 2: Fall asleep.

Fig. 3: Note the time the falling spoon wakes you.

Fig. 4: Calculate the difference between bedtime and the spoon dropping.

7. In the morning, calculate the difference between the time when you got into bed and the time when you woke up to the sound of the spoon **(fig. 4)**. This difference in time is your sleep latency. For example, if you got into bed at 9:05 p.m. and the spoon woke you up at 9:21 p.m., then it took you 16 minutes to fall asleep.

THINKING DEEPER
Most people fall asleep 10 to 20 minutes after they turn off the lights and get into bed. If people fall asleep too fast, it may mean that they are not getting enough sleep. People who have trouble falling asleep may have trouble relaxing, feel anxious, or have jet lag. Drinking too much coffee or other drinks with caffeine can also affect a person's ability to fall asleep and the quality of sleep. Investigate how your mood and behavior affect your sleep latency. Before you go to sleep, record how you feel and when you have consumed anything with caffeine during the day (such as soda or chocolate). Measure your sleep latency and compare the time it took you to fall asleep when you were in different moods and when you consumed different amounts of caffeine.

WHAT'S GOING ON?
As you fall asleep, your muscles will relax and the spoon will fall out of your hand. The noise of the spoon hitting the plate should wake you up. Of course, if the spoon misses the plate, you may not wake up. If this happens, provide a larger target area for the spoon, such as a large metal cookie sheet.

BRAIN FACTS

→ Normal body temperature for humans is 98.6°F (37°C), but it can vary by about 2°F (1°C) depending on the time of day.

→ Normal body temperature for dogs is 101.5°F (38.6°C).

→ Heat stroke happens when a person becomes too hot and hypothermia happens when a person becomes too cold.

All animals have a built-in clock that controls their behavior. Body rhythms that keep a daily pattern are called circadian rhythms. One circadian rhythm that is easy to track is your own body temperature.

⏰ Time

→ 5 minutes several times a day

🔑 Materials

→ Digital thermometer
→ Pen or pencil
→ Lab notebook
→ Graph paper

⚠ Safety Tips

→ Do not use a thermometer that has liquid in it.
→ Make sure you know how to use a digital thermometer properly.
→ Wash the thermometer carefully after each use.

Fig. 1: Measure your temperature every 2 hours.

📝 Method

1. When you wake up, place a digital thermometer under your tongue to measure your body temperature. Record the time of day and your temperature in your lab notebook.

2. Measure your temperature every 2 hours from the time you get up in the morning until the time you go to sleep **(fig. 1)**. If you cannot measure your temperature every 2 hours, then just measure it as often as possible.

3. Do not eat or drink anything right before you take your temperature. Make sure to take your temperature the same way each time **(fig. 2)**.

Fig. 2: Take temperature same way every time.

Fig. 3: Record your body temperature.

4. After you have collected a full day of data **(fig. 3)**, plot the recorded temperatures on graph paper **(fig. 4)**. The time of day should be on the *x*-axis and body temperature should be on the *y*-axis.

Fig. 4: Chart your body temperature.

WHAT'S GOING ON?

A person's body temperature usually shows a daily cycle. Most people have their highest body temperature in the afternoon and lowest body temperature in the very early morning. Body temperature is also dependent on a person's age, activity, and stress level.

The area of the brain called the hypothalamus helps regulate body temperature. The hypothalamus receives information about skin temperature and has its own sensors that detect the temperature of blood. The hypothalamus can send signals throughout the body to control sweating, shivering, and the diameter of blood vessels to keep body temperature within normal range. If skin temperature is low, the hypothalamus sends signals automatically to stop sweating, reduce blood flow to the skin, and start shivering. If a person gets too hot, then the hypothalamus sends messages to start sweating and increase blood flow to the skin.

THINKING DEEPER

Combine this body temperature lab with the Lab 14: Catch Me If You Can. Measure your reaction time to catching the ruler and plot your "catch times" with your body temperature. Is there a correlation between body temperature and reaction time?

Sleep and Body Rhythms

BRAIN FACTS

→ The word *circadian* comes from the Latin word meaning "about a day."

→ The suprachiasmatic nucleus contains about 20,000 neurons.

→ Jet lag occurs when circadian rhythms are disrupted.

Track the rhythm of activity of an animal throughout the day.

⏰ Time

→ **All day**

🔑 Materials

→ **Research subject (dog, cat, fish, or other animal)**
→ **Clock**
→ **Lab notebook**
→ **Pencil**
→ **Timer**
→ **Graph paper**

📝 Method

1. Decide what animal will be your research subject. A pet will make a good subject because you will be able to observe it for a long time **(fig. 1)**.

2. Every 2 hours (more often if you like), observe your research subject for 5 minutes **(fig. 2)**.

3. In your lab notebook, record the time of day when you make your observations.

Fig. 1: Study an animal like a fish to watch for cycling patterns.

4. Use the timer to measure the amount of time your research subject spends doing different behaviors within a 5-minute period. For example, your subject might spend 1 minute drinking water and 4 minutes walking around, or it may spend all 5 minutes sleeping.

5. In your notebook, record the amount of time your subject spends doing each behavior.

6. Do not disturb your subject while you are observing it.

Fig. 2: Check on it every 2 hours.

Fig. 3: Chart the amount of time spent on each behavior.

Fig. 4: What other animals could you observe?

7. Graph the amount of time spent in each behavior at different times of the day **(fig. 3)**. The *x*-axis of your graph should be the time of day and the *y*-axis should be the time spent in different behaviors.

8. Keep an activity record for several days **(fig. 4)**.

WHAT'S GOING ON?

In this lab, you studied animal behavior in a natural setting. This type of research is called naturalistic observation. By examining the graphs you made, you will likely find that some behaviors are more common at some times of the day. Animal behaviors follow a regular pattern called circadian rhythms. A common circadian rhythm is sleep, but hormones, neurotransmitters, heart rate, hunger, and body temperature also show regular patterns every 24 hours.

The suprachiasmatic nucleus, a part of the hypothalamus, is an area of the brain critical for coordinating all circadian rhythms. This brain area receives signals from the eyes. Light from the Sun is important for regulating the activity of the suprachiasmatic nucleus and setting the internal body clock every day. In addition to light, exercise, stress, drugs, and other factors can influence daily activity rhythms.

THINKING DEEPER

Are you a morning lark or a night owl? In other words, do you feel alert and ready to go in the morning or do you feel best at night? Track your level of alertness by recording how you feel each hour. Give yourself a score of 3 if you feel attentive and alert or a 1 if you feel tired and unfocused. Record a score of 2 if you feel somewhere between attentive and tired.

UNIT 10

MEMORY

YOUR MEMORIES MAKE YOU who you are. They tell you the who, what, when, where, and why of your life. Without your old memories and the ability to make new memories, you would find it very difficult to go about your daily life.

Memories are created over time in a three-stage process. First, information is stored in sensory receptors for less than 1 second. If you pay attention, this information is passed into short-term (working) memory. The capacity of short-term memory is limited because it can hold only a few items at a time. However, if the information in short-term memory is repeated and given meaning, it can enter long-term memory for permanent storage.

Long-term memories have two basic types: declarative memories and procedural memories. Declarative memories are memories for names, facts, and dates. Procedural memories are memories for skills such as riding a bike or shooting a basketball. We know that the brain stores declarative memories and procedural memories differently because people with brain damage might have trouble with one type of memory but not the other.

In the following labs, you will investigate how memories are formed and recalled. The labs will let you explore short-term memory for things you see, hear, and feel. You will also attempt to influence the memory of other people. These labs should show that memory can be improved and that it can change over time.

NOW YOU SEE IT, NOW YOU DON'T

BRAIN FACTS

→ Short-term memory is also called working memory.

→ Retrograde amnesia is memory loss for events that happened before an injury; anterograde amnesia is the inability to form new memories.

→ People with Alzheimer's disease have gradual memory loss and difficulty remembering new information.

Test your short-term memory with common objects.

Fig. 1: Scatter 10 to 20 items on a tray or plate.

Fig. 2: Cover the items with a cloth or napkin.

⏰ Time
→ 30 minutes

🪝 Materials
→ 20 small items (such as an eraser, pencil, coin, marble, etc.)
→ Tray or plate
→ Cloth or towel to cover the tray
→ Timer
→ Paper and pencils for your subjects

📝 Method

1. Place the objects on the tray (**fig. 1**).

2. Cover the tray with a cloth (**fig. 2**).

3. Explain to your test subjects that you want them to remember as many objects on the tray as possible in 1 minute (**fig. 3**).

Fig. 3: Let subjects memorize what's on the tray for 1 minute.

Fig. 4: Cover the tray, have them turn around, and remove one item.

Fig. 5: Ask your test subjects to turn back around and tell you which item was removed.

4. Remove the towel or cloth from the tray and start the timer.

5. After 1 minute, cover the tray and ask your test subjects to write down all of the items that they can remember.

THINKING DEEPER

In this lab, you used only twenty objects. Make the test more difficult by adding more objects to remember or by reducing the amount of time you give your test subjects to memorize the objects. Also, check to see whether any of the objects made it into the long-term memory of your test subjects by checking their recall one day, one week, or one month after they first memorized the objects. Another way to use this lab is to ask your test subjects to memorize the objects and then remove one or more objects from the tray **(fig. 4)**. Now, show your test subjects the tray of objects and ask whether they know which object is missing **(fig. 5)**.

This lab can also be used to test the ability to remember objects using the sense of touch. To do this, use Lab 34: The Little Box of Science with twenty objects. Your test subjects should never see any of the objects. To memorize the objects, your test subjects should place their hands inside the box to feel the objects. Compare the ability to memorize objects using vision versus touch.

WHAT'S GOING ON?

To remember something, you must first pay attention. This transfers information to short-term memory. Without repetition and rehearsal, information stays in short-term memory for only a brief time, perhaps 10 to 20 seconds. Also, the amount of information is limited. Some research shows that only about seven items can be held in short-term memory at any one time.

The area of the brain called the hippocampus is critical for getting short-term memories into long-term memory. People with damage to the hippocampus can remember events that just happened, but will forget things if they are not continually repeated. If a memory is stored before the hippocampus is damaged, then the memory will not be lost.

NEURO-TELEPHONE

BRAIN FACTS

→ Déjà vu is the feeling that something that just happened also occurred in the past.

→ Adequate sleep is essential for moving memories into long-term memory.

→ Dory, the fish in the movie *Finding Nemo*, had anterograde amnesia: she could not form new memories.

How is your memory for words? Find out by playing a game of neuro-telephone.

Fig. 1: Once in a circle, one person starts by saying a word.

Fig. 2: The next person adds a word and keeps going around the circle.

⏰ Time
→ 30 minutes

🖋 Materials
→ A group of test subjects

📝 Method

1. Arrange a group of test subjects in a circle. One person should say a single word about the brain, nerve cell, or senses. For example, this person could say "neuron" **(fig. 1).**

2. The second person must then say "neuron" and then add a new brain word, such as "retina" **(fig. 2).**

3. The third person must say "neuron, retina" and add another word, such as "cortex."

4. The game continues until someone forgets a word in the list.

THINKING DEEPER

Instead of using brainy words in this lab, use words that are more common or use numbers, letters, and colors. You can even repeat words that have already been said to make the game more difficult.

WHAT'S GOING ON?

This lab investigates auditory memory. Auditory memory involves the ability to hear sounds, process this information, keep the information, and then recall it. Sounds enter the ear where receptors send electrical signals to the brain. The brain must understand these signals, store the information, and then recall it when necessary.

Each time a new word is added to a neuro-telephone list, the brain must store additional information. Repeating the words helps keep the information in short-term memory. However, short-term memory has a limited capacity and cannot store too many words.

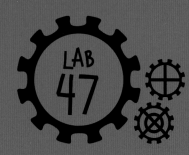

LAB 47

MEMORY IMPLANT

BRAIN FACTS

→ Neuroscientists sometime provide expert testimony during courtroom proceedings to give their opinions about the memory of a witness.

→ Researchers are working to develop a drug that would remove specific memories.

→ Moderate exercise can reduce the risk of developing Alzheimer's disease, a brain disorder that causes memory problems.

Sometimes, your brain makes up its own memories. In this lab, you will implant a memory into someone else.

Fig. 1: Read the list of words.

⏰ Time
→ 30 minutes

🪝 Materials
→ Word list (opposite)

📝 Method
1. Tell your test subjects that you want them to remember a list of twenty words that you will read.

Fig. 2: Wait 5 minutes.

Fig. 3: Ask if they remember the word "sleep."

2. Read the following list of words (about one word per second) to your test subjects **(fig. 1)**:

> bed   pillow   blanket   nighttime   mattress   time   dream   room
> tired   sheets   drowsy   rest   dark   clock   nap   snooze   quiet
> doze   crib   yawn

3. Wait for 5 minutes **(fig. 2)** and then ask your test subjects whether they remember the word *clock* on the list. Did they remember the word *dream*? Did they remember the word *sleep* **(fig. 3)**?

THINKING DEEPER

Make your own list of words to create a false memory in someone. Your list could be about a sport, holiday, or place. The list should have at least twenty words.

WHAT'S GOING ON?

Your test subjects will likely say that they remember the words *clock, dream,* and *sleep.* But which words were really on the list? Only *clock* and *dream* were on the list. The word *sleep* was not on the list. Therefore, listening to words about sleep implanted the memory that the word *sleep* was on the list.

This lab shows that memories are not stored in the brain like information on a computer or voice recorder. Rather, memory can be influenced by other events and information that the brain receives. Memories can also be altered as time passes. For example, details of events that happened in the past may be difficult to recall and you might be uncertain about what really occurred. This is especially important to judges, lawyers, and juries who must weigh the testimony of eyewitnesses when deciding a court case.

NOW OR LATER

BRAIN FACTS

→ Mnemonics are memory tricks that help you remember information. For example, the name "ROY G. BIV" is an easy way to remember the colors in the visible spectrum: red (R), orange (O), yellow (Y), green (G), blue (B), indigo (I), and violet (V).

→ "Chunking" is a memory strategy that groups several items into a single unit. For example, eight separate numbers, 16452013, can be reduced to just two: 1645 and 2013.

Investigate how the order in which you hear a list of words affects your ability to remember the words.

⏰ Time

→ 30 minutes

🚀 Materials

→ Word list (below)
→ Paper and pencils for your test subjects

📝 Method

1. Tell your test subjects that you will read a list of words and that their job is to remember as many of the words as possible.

2. Read the following list of twenty words to your test subjects at a rate of one word every second **(fig. 1)**.

cat apple ball tree square
head house door box car
king hammer milk fish
book tape arrow flower
key shoe

Fig. 1: Read the list of words.

3. When you are finished reading the list, ask your test subjects to write down the words that they can remember **(fig. 2)**.

4. Collect the lists of words that your subjects remembered.

5. Analyze the data by assigning a "position" to each word that you read. The first word (cat) should get a "1" and the next word (apple) should get a "2," and so on.

6. Graph how many times each word was remembered by all of your test subjects **(fig. 3)**.

Fig. 2: Have listeners write down words they remember.

Fig. 3: Plot results.

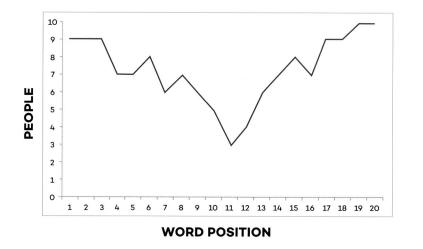

WORD POSITION

7. The graph above shows an example of a serial-position curve. The *x*-axis is the position of each word and the *y*-axis is the number of people who remembered each word. In this example, nine people remembered the first three words, but only seven people remembered the fourth word on the list.

WHAT'S GOING ON?

This experiment usually results in a graph similar to the one on this page. This kind of graph is called a serial-position curve. Words read first and words read last are remembered better than words read in the middle of a list. The serial-position curve shows that there are two types of memory. One is good for the words read last because they are still in short-term memory. This is called the recency effect because the words were heard most recently. Memory is also good for the words read first because they made it into long-term memory. This is called the primacy effect.

Some words in the list may have been easy for some people to recall because they have special meaning. For example, if someone has a pet fish and heard the word *fish*, they might remember this word because they think of their pet.

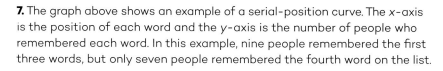

THINKING DEEPER

If your test subjects can remember all twenty words, then make the lab more difficult by adding ten more words to the list. You should experiment with distraction with a new group of test subjects. For example, read the same list of words, but distract them immediately after you finish reading the list by asking them to count backward from one hundred by threes for 15 to 30 seconds. Graph your results and look for differences between the undistracted group and the distracted group.

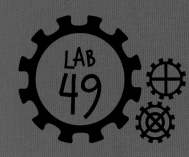

GROCERY STORE

BRAIN FACTS

→ Strong memories of the past can often be triggered by specific smells associated with an event that took place a long time ago.

→ Strong memories are often formed when an event causes strong emotions.

→ A blow to the head will not restore memories to someone with amnesia.

The next time you go to the store, you may not need a list because you will have memorized it.

⏰ Time
→ 30 minutes

🔑 Materials
→ Pencil or pen
→ Paper

✏️ Method

1. Before you go to the store, make a shopping list of food you need to buy **(fig. 1)**.

2. Memorize the items on the list by reading them several times.

3. Take the list with you to the store **(fig. 2)**.

4. When you are at the store, shop by recalling the items on the list without looking at the list **(fig. 3)**.

Fig. 3: Shop by recalling a list.

5. When you are finished shopping, but before you leave the store, check the list **(fig. 4)** to make sure you did not forget anything.

Fig. 1: Make a list.

Fig. 2: Take the list with you but don't look at it.

Fig. 4: Check the list. Did you remember everything?

THINKING DEEPER

"Chaining" is a memory strategy that can help you remember a list of words. This method requires that you make mental pictures of the words and then connect them. The best connecting mental pictures are ones that are strange. Let's suppose that the first four items on a shopping list are apples, bread, tomato sauce, and eggs. A strange mental picture could be of four apples forming the legs of a tabletop made from a slice of bread. The next mental images might be of bread pieces wrapped around a jar of tomato sauce and tomato cans breaking eggs. All you have to do is remember the first word on the list to bring back the images of the other words.

WHAT'S GOING ON?

Did you remember everything on your shopping list? Rehearsing or repeating the list of words helps transfer short-term memories into long-term memories, but it is possible that you forgot some of the items. Some scientists think we forget because new information interferes with old information. Forgetting may also happen when a memory pathway in the brain is lost. It is possible that a memory is still in the brain, but it is just difficult to recall.

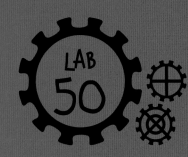

LAB 50

WORD MEMORY

BRAIN FACTS

→ The average twenty-year-old native speaker of American English knows about 42,000 words.[7]

→ Simon Reinhard holds the world record for remembering random words; in 2010, he recalled 300 words correctly after studying them for 15 minutes.

[7]M. Brysbaert, M. Stevens, P. Mandera, and E. Keuleers, "How Many Words Do We Know? Practical Estimates of Vocabulary Size Dependent on Word Definition, the Degree of Language Input and the Participant's Age." *Frontiers in Psychology* 7 (2016): 1116.

Some words are easier to remember than other words, especially if they are difficult to picture in your mind. In this lab, you will test the ability to remember concrete, abstract, and nonsense words.

Fig. 1: Read words to test subject. Ask them to write down words they remember.

⏰ Time

→ 30 minutes

🖋 Materials

→ **Word lists (opposite)**
→ **Paper and pencils for test subjects**

🖊 Method

1. Tell your test subjects that you will read them a list of words and they should try to remember as many as they can (**fig. 1**).

2. Read the list of concrete words to your test subjects at a rate of one word each second (**fig. 2**).

Fig. 3: Read abstract words.

Fig. 4: Do they remember as many?

3. After you finish reading the list, ask your test subjects to write down as many words as they can remember **(fig. 3)**. Concrete word list:

apple   window   baby   bird   shoes   butterfly   pencil   corn   flower   belt
hammer   house   money   chair   ocean   car   rock   book   table   arrow

4. Read this list of abstract words to your test subjects at a rate of one word each second and then ask your test subjects to write down as many words as they can remember. Abstract word list:

anger   mercy   boredom   theory   hope   effort   fate   freedom   justice
happiness   honor   concept   idea   interest   knowledge   belief   mood
moral   chance   truth

5. Read this list of nonsense words to your test subjects at a rate of one word each second and then ask your test subjects to write down as many words as they can remember. Nonsense word list:

vobec   botam   crov   leptav   kayrim   glimoc   ricul   hilbom
sowin   kepwin   difim   cumal   mib   natpem   girap
rispaw   jolib   tubiv   ator   yapib

6. Count the number of words on each list that your test subjects remembered **(fig. 4)**.

WHAT'S GOING ON?

Most people find that words that have a real physical structure (concrete words) are easier to remember than words that are difficult to picture (abstract words and nonsense words). Concreteness refers to the ability of a word to form a mental image. For example, everyone knows what an apple looks like, but they may not be able to form a mental image of the word *truth*. The meaning of a word also contributes to how well a word can be remembered. Nonsense words have no meaning and are more difficult to remember than concrete words and abstract words.

THINKING DEEPER

Create your own lists of words to investigate what other characteristics of words make them memorable. For example, make a list of long words with more than one syllable and another list of short words with only one syllable. Which list is more difficult to remember?

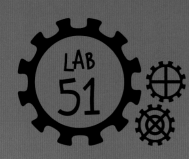
LOCATION³

BRAIN FACTS

→ The word *hippocampus* comes from the Greek words meaning "horse" and "sea monster" because this brain structure resembles a seahorse.

→ London taxi drivers, who have extensive knowledge of the streets and locations of London, have a larger than average hippocampus.[8]

[8] E. A. Maguire, K. Woollett, and H. J. Spiers, "London Taxi Drivers and Bus Drivers: A Structural MRI and Neuropsychological Analysis." *Hippocampus* 16 (2006): 1091–1101.

Test your memory for places using this lab.

Fig. 1: Mark off a large, open area with chalk, tape, or cones.

⏰ Time
→ 30 minutes

🔑 Materials
→ Chalk or rope
→ Blindfold
→ Tennis ball
→ Timer

✍ Method

1. Find a large, open area or room without obstacles.

2. Mark a large playing area with chalk, tape, or plastic cones **(fig. 1)**.

3. Blindfold your test subject **(fig. 2)**.

4. Place the tennis ball somewhere within the playing area **(fig. 3)**.

5. Ask your test subject to find the tennis ball **(fig. 4)**.

6. Say, "Go" to begin the test and start the timer.

7. If you're indoors, make sure that your test subject does not bump into any furniture or the wall.

8. When your test subject finds the ball, stop the timer. Record the amount of time it took to find the ball.

9. Put your test subject back into the same starting location.

10. Place the tennis ball in the same place as the first time.

11. Have your test subject find the ball again and record the amount of time it took to find the ball **(fig. 5)**.

Fig. 2: Blindfold a test subject.

Fig. 3: Place a tennis ball within the playing area.

Fig. 4: Ask the subject to find the ball and record how long it takes.

Fig. 5: Put subject and ball in the same places and repeat the experiment.

12. Repeat the experiment several times and then compare the time it took to find the ball on the different tries. Plot the results of the experiment on a graph with the trial number on the x-axis and the time to find the ball on the y-axis.

WHAT'S GOING ON?

The amount of time your test subject took to find the ball should have decreased with more trials. The ability to remember locations is called spatial memory. As people explore their environments, they make mental maps of the space. The hippocampus and parts of the cerebral cortex are areas of the brain that are used when these maps are made.

THINKING DEEPER

Collect ten different small objects, such as a coin, a paper clip, a rock, an eraser, and a pencil. Hide the objects around your house. Make a list of the objects and their locations. Place the list in an envelope and put the envelope in a safe place. Wait at least a week and then try to find the hidden objects. If you cannot locate all of the objects, open the envelope and read your list.

CONCENTRATION

BRAIN FACTS

→ Leonardo da Vinci (1452–1519) is credited with an amazing ability to remember faces and to draw them accurately after seeing a person only once.

→ A "tip-of-the-tongue" experience occurs when you feel you know an answer, but cannot quite remember it.

Play the game of concentration to test your ability to remember location.

⏰ Time

→ 1 hour

✂ Materials

→ Scissors
→ Cardboard
→ Ruler
→ 2 copies of the same picture
→ Glue

📝 Method

1. To make a set of playing cards, cut the cardboard into rectangles 2¾ by 2 inches (7 by 5 cm).

2. Print out two copies of the same picture.

3. Glue the pictures to the cardboard pieces and then let them dry **(fig. 1)**.

4. Make twenty pairs (forty cards total) of cards.

5. To set up the game, mix the cards.

Fig. 4: Use your memory to find matches.

6. Make a grid of eight cards by five cards with the cards face down so you cannot see the pictures **(fig. 2)**.

7. To play the game, one person should turn over one card. Then the same person should turn over one more card **(fig. 3)**. If the pictures on the two cards are the same, that player picks up those two cards and has another turn.

Fig. 1: Glue duplicated pictures to cardboard squares.

Fig. 2: Make an eight-by-five grid with the cards.

Fig. 3: Take turns turning over cards.

8. If the pictures on the cards are not the same, the person puts the cards, face down, back in the same place where they were found.

9. The next player should then have a turn to find matching pictures.

10. The object of the game is to remember where a particular card is located and to find as many matching cards as possible **(fig. 4)**.

 11. The person with the most matching cards is the winner.

WHAT'S GOING ON?

To find a matching card, the location of the first card is kept in short-term memory and long-term memory. Accurate memory is important if a card is turned over early in the game but its matching card is not located until later in the game. Players must remember the initial location of the card to find its match.

THINKING DEEPER

To make the game more difficult, make more cards to increase the size of the grid. You can also use different pictures of the same thing. For example, you could make a pair of cards with two different dogs. Even though the cards have pictures of two different dogs, the cards would still be a match. Try the game with words on the cards instead of pictures. Is it easier or more difficult to remember the locations of words?

RESOURCES

📘 Books

Chudler, E. H. *Inside Your Brain.*
New York: Chelsea House Publishers, 2007.

Chudler, E. H. *The Little Book of Neuroscience Haiku.*
New York: W. W. Norton & Company, 2013.

Chudler, E. H., and L. A. Johnson.
*Brain Bytes: Quick Answers to Curious
Questions about the Brain.*
New York: W. W. Norton & Company, 2017.

Eagleman, D. *The Brain: The Story of You.*
New York: Pantheon Books, 2015.

Farinella, M., and H. Ros. *Neurocomic.*
London: Nobrow Ltd., 2013.

Fleischman, J. *Phineas Gage: A Gruesome
but True Story about Brain Science.*
Boston: Houghton Mifflin Co., 2002.

Swanson, L. W., E. Newman, A. Araque, and
J. M. Dubinsky. *The Beautiful Brain:
The Drawings of Santiago Ramon y Cajal.*
New York: Abrams, 2017.

 Websites

The Brain from Top to Bottom:
http://thebrain.mcgill.ca

BrainU, Cool Stuff:
http://brainu.org/cool-stuff

BrainWorks:
http://uwtv.org/series/brainworks

Comparative Mammalian Brain Collections:
http://brainmuseum.org

Knowing Neurons:
http://knowingneurons.com

National Institute on Drug Abuse:
www.drugabuse.gov

Neuroscience for Kids:
http://faculty.washington.edu/chudler/neurok.html

Society for Neuroscience:
www.sfn.org

Your Amazing Brain:
www.youramazingbrain.org.uk

APPENDIX

Measurement Conversions

DISTANCE
1 micron = 1000 nanometers
1 mm = 1000 microns
1 cm = 10 mm = 0.4 inch
1 m = 100 cm = 3.3 ft
1 km = 1000 m = 0.6 mile

SPEED
1 m/s = 3.6 km/hr = 2.2 mile/hr
120 m/s = 432 km/hr = 268 mile/hr

VOLUME
10 ml = 2 teaspoons
75 ml = 5 tablespoons
100 ml = 0.4 cup
200 ml = 0.8 cup
250 ml = 1 cup

TEMPERATURE
37°C = 98.6°F
175°C = 350°F

WEIGHT
50 gm = 0.1 lb = 1.8 oz
270 gm = 0.6 lb
400 gm = 0.9 lb
1.4 kg = 3.1 lb

Sarah

 Claire

 Sophia

 Max

 Wyatt

 Annika

 Ingrid

 Katy

 Maeve

 Sarah

 Alessa

 Mia

 Carissa

 Kyra

 Avery

 Abigail

 Roshan

 Anja

 Mayzelle

 Ai-Quynh

 Alison

 Elliot

 Huxley

 Lakken

 Giada

 Grady

 Koy

 Evan

 Grace

 Marie

 Charlie

 Ella

 Avelaine

 Simon

 Ani

 Lydia

 Easton

 Scarlett

 Isaac

 May

 Enzo

ACKNOWLEDGMENTS

THANK YOU to my wife, Sandy, and kids, Kelly and Sam, for tolerating messy kitchen tabletops and cluttered shelves as I developed the experiments and activities in this book. I hope you enjoyed testing the activities before anyone else used the materials.

My gratitude goes out to the editors at Quarry Books, Jonathan Simcosky and John Gettings, who helped guide *Brain Lab for Kids* through the publication process. Their patience and thoughtful answers to my many questions are appreciated.

Finally, Liz Heinecke, the fantastic photographer, and all of the children who appear in the book must be acknowledged for their time and effort to bring color and life to the book.

ABOUT THE AUTHOR

ERIC H. CHUDLER is a research neuroscientist interested in how the brain processes information from the senses, especially from the skin. He is currently investigating how chemicals in medicinal plants and herbs affect the nervous system and regeneration. Eric received his Ph.D. from the Department of Psychology at the University of Washington in Seattle in 1985. He has worked at the National Institutes of Health in Bethesda, MD, (1986–1989) and in the Department of Neurosurgery at Massachusetts General Hospital in Boston, MA, (1989–1991). He is currently a research associate professor in the Department of Bioengineering and the executive director/education director at the Center for Sensorimotor Neural Engineering. He is also a faculty member in both the Department of Anesthesiology & Pain Medicine and the Graduate Program of Neurobiology and Behavior at the University of Washington. In addition to performing basic neuroscience research, Eric works with other neuroscientists and classroom teachers to develop educational materials to help students learn about the brain.

INDEX

ALSO AVAILABLE

**KITCHEN SCIENCE
LAB FOR KIDS**
978-1-59253-925-3

**OUTDOOR SCIENCE
LAB FOR KIDS**
978-1-63159-115-0

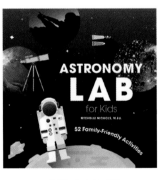

**ASTRONOMY
LAB FOR KIDS**
978-1-63159-134-1

**ENERGY
LAB FOR KIDS**
978-1-63159-250-8